Trust
Your
Gut!

Trust
Your
Gut!

Practical Ways to Develop and Use Your Intuition for Business Success

Richard M. Contino

American Management Association

New York • Atlanta • Boston • Chicago • Kansas City • San Francisco • Washington, D.C.
Brussels • Mexico City • Tokyo • Toronto

This publication is designed to provide accurate and authoritative information in regard to the subject matter covered. It is sold with the understanding that the publisher is not engaged in rendering legal, accounting, or other professional service. If legal advice or other expert assistance is required, the services of a competent professional person should be sought.

Library of Congress Cataloging-in-Publication Data

Contino, Richard M.
    Trust your gut! : practical ways to develop and use your intuition
/ Richard M. Contino.
      p. cm.
    Includes bibliographical references and index.
    ISBN 0-8144-7877-8
    1. Success in business.   2. Intuition (Psychology)   3. Executives-
-Psychology.   I. Title.
    HF5386.C749   1996
    153.4'4—dc20
                                     96–17190
                                         CIP

Printing number

10 9 8 7 6 5 4 3 2 1

To
**Penelope,
May-Lynne,
Matthew,**
and
my **Mother**

Contents

Introduction

The economic downturn of the late 1980s and early 1990s put unparalleled pressures on businesspeople to find new ways to survive and prosper. To make it, or even survive, in the today's work world, new skills, approaches, philosophies, and attitudes are required. This is something Peter Senge, the director of The Center for Organizational Learning at Massachusetts Institute of Technology's renown Sloan School of Management, aptly points out in his revolutionary management book, *The Fifth Discipline: The Art and Practice of the Learning Organization*, and reinforces in its 1994 sequel, *The Fifth Discipline Fieldbook: Strategies and Tools for Building a Learning Organization*. Senge, along with many other business visionaries, emphatically states that our life in business must be a continual learning process, and we must go beyond traditional job performance requirements and develop solid personal skills to be able to effectively communicate, listen, and manage our self-destructive emotions. And we must learn to use our intuition.

History is filled with stories of people who have used their intuition to solve business problems, generate new ideas, create business or career success realities, and predict decision outcomes. Edwin Land's story about how he came up with the concept for the Polaroid camera is legendary. Land was vacationing with his family in Santa Fe in 1943. He had just taken a picture of his daughter, Jennifer, with a conventional camera, when she asked him why she could not immediately see the picture. Land was intrigued, but had no answers. Suddenly, about an hour later, the complete methodology for the design and operation of this revolutionary camera flashed into his mind.

Steve Jobs, the founder of Apple Computer, and a business visionary, followed his intuition and created a major industry. Jobs sensed there was a market for small personal computers. He approached major computer manufacturers with his vision of the computing future, hoping to enlist their support. Every manufacturer turned him down, telling him that, based on their market research, facts, and figures, there was no market for personal computers. Jobs trusted his gut feeling. He developed the Apple computer, and revolutionized the computing industry. Today, personal computers are a multi-billion dollar industry. And still growing.

You can also use your intuition for business success. And *Trust Your Gut!* will be your guide. Imagine for a moment the possibilities if you had access to a powerful inner mentor that could help you navigate the raging rapids of the business world—to help you find innovative solutions to tough problems, originate new market new ideas, uncover hidden agendas, handle difficult people, or make more successful career or business choices. Well, if you're willing to suspend all negative thoughts, doubts, and other self-imposed limitations for a few hours, be prepared to have this become a reality by simply allowing a natural inner capability to surface: your intuitive ability.

In the pages that follow, you will learn about your intuitive potential and how you can develop it. To do so, however, you must be ready to journey a road that you may never have traveled, to explore ways of thinking you may never have considered, and to risk a few wrong turns as you fine-tune your emerging intuitive capabilities. Although the learning process is non-traditional, never doubt for one moment that your intuition is not a serious, effective, and powerful skill for business.

The mind-expanding techniques for releasing your intuitive abilities offered in *Trust Your Gut!* are based on my fifteen-year search for ways to predictably increase business success. Even with an extensive educational background in engineering, law, business, and finance, it quickly became clear that more was required. And it was also apparent that it was not something you could learn in business school or from business books. So, in my efforts to make solid headway as a Wall Street attorney and businessman, I actively sought the advice and insights of business leaders, mentors, entrepreneurs, and management consultants. There were no set formulas. There were no set answers. A life-changing breakthrough came, however, when I decided to leave the security of a mainstream career path to purse a direction that intellectually made no sense, but "felt" right. Everyone, including me at moments along the way, thought the decision was not only a mistake, but self-destructive. As it turned out, it was the best business decision I had ever made. And one that would forever better my career progress. And it was the genesis for a commitment to understanding and honing my intuitive ability as a business success tool.

Developing your intuition for business is easy—once the mystery is taken out of the process. It is not a paranormal or mystical power. It's a capability you were born with—and, if you're not using its full potential, one that you're probably ignoring or repressing. To access your intuition, you don't have to be in an altered state of consciousness, engage in mental contortions, or undergo a mystical or magical experience. Removing unfounded and self-imposed mental and emotional roadblocks is all that's required. So, with an open mind, some guidance, and practice, you can add it to *your* business tool kit. *Trust Your Gut!* will show you how.

Book Approach

This book is divided into three parts. In Part One, you will learn about intuition, your innate intuitive potential, what you can do to make an intuition skill breakthrough, what to expect as your skill is developing, and how to identify your intuitive style. Once you know the basics, Part Two will systematically lead you through six steps necessary for removing all blocks, such as negative thoughts, self-doubts, anxieties, fears, and life illusions, to the natural flow of your intuitive information. You'll then be shown how to ensure and accelerate your developmental progress. With all this under your belt, you'll be shown, in Part Three, how to apply and hone your emerging ability with techniques for business, so that using your intuition becomes an effortless and natural part of your business assessment and decision-making process.

At each key development stage, you'll have concrete exercises or techniques to enable you to measure your progress, and facilitate and hone your intuition for business. One more thought to keep in mind as you read: This is not a book of theory that you must accept at face value, but one that offers developmental tools that will enable you to explore the power of your intuitive mind, and release its potential. So, relax, experiment, and have fun.

Acknowledgments

I wish to express my appreciation to everyone who has been of assistance in bringing this book to fruition. In particular, I wish to thank my agent, Jeff Herman, for trusting his gut on the book idea; my acquisitions editor, Mary Glenn, for her key business insights in keeping the book on track; and my developmental editor, Jacqueline Flynn, for her beyond-the-call-of-duty commitment in bringing the manuscript ideas into sharp focus.

My special thanks to my wonderful wife, and silent co-author, Penelope, for graciously putting up with my absence during the many hours it took to write this book, her moral support when I got bogged down, and, above all, lending her outstanding professional writing talents to this book; to my delightful eight-year-old daughter, May-Lynne, for keeping my writing office cheerful with her many beautiful and colorful paintings and her fine executive assistance in handling telephone calls while I was working; to our newborn, Matthew, for sleeping through the night—well, almost—in the last months of the writing process; and, finally, to my dear mother for burning the midnight oil to give me her fine editorial input.

Part One:

Intuition for Business:
The Basics

Chapter 1

Intuition and Business

"My Intuition leads me."
—Peter W.,
business pioneer,
industry leader

Without a doubt, you are aware of an innate ability called intuition, an intangible experience that is hard to put into words.
The dictionary defines *intuition* as "the power of knowing;
knowledge without recourse to reason; innate or instinctive
knowledge; a quick or ready apprehension." You have heard
others speak of hunches, gut feelings, a sense of knowing, an
inner compass that guides how you make decisions from time
to time, or a foreboding that inexplicably foreshadows unhappiness; you may even have spoken of these things yourself. The
women among you and around you might even describe themselves as being intuitive. More than their male counterparts,
they tend to admit that they rely on intuition to read others or
to evaluate situations.

Intuition: An Art Not a Science

Intuition is a source of knowledge, of hidden knowledge. We are
not quite sure of its origin, and deploying it seems more of an art
than a science. Perhaps it is for these reasons that as level-head-
ed people managing our lives, specifically our business lives, we
resist relying on what we might consider an unreliable tool. I

would wager that few readers count their intuition as a major resource that if followed can time and again lead to favorable outcomes, but it is.

Throughout this book, I will invite you to explore your intuition—to recognize it, develop it, and strengthen it. I will teach you how to overcome your own skepticism about putting your intuition to work in business, and how to eliminate the obstacles that distort or inhibit your progress in building your intuitive skills. You will hear accounts from other business professionals. Some trust their intuition and reap the rewards. Others want more access to it, but are uncertain about how to accomplish this, and wonder if they should even try. You may recognize yourself in their stories. Reading this book will take you on a journey. Your destination is that place where you will fully understand what your intuition is and what it can do for you, especially in the business arena. Hopefully, by journey's end, you will be ready, willing, and able to put your intuition to work as an important addition to your business arsenal.

A Powerful Business Tool

Today more than ever, you must take advantage of every available resource if you are to survive, let alone succeed, in business. Corporate America is restructuring and downsizing, the job marketplace continues to change dramatically, with limited openings for many traditional jobs, and consumer needs and interests are shifting. It has been a time of high frustration and uncertainty, and of reduced earning potential. Making the right choices, steering your course in business, has never been so important.

For most people in business, intuition, a powerful inner instinct, is a little-cultivated resource that if used effectively could make the difference between success and failure. Hard to believe? Well, imagine for a moment the competitive edge that could be yours if you could quickly solve business problems, identify new market opportunities, uncover your opponent's hidden negotiating agenda, and consistently make successful business decisions. These are exciting thoughts. Developing your intuitive ability can make them exciting realities.

More successful people than you might think often rely heavily on their intuition. Describing his intuitive approach to business, Peter W., a prominent international financial services executive, says:

> "I use my intuition about 90 percent of the time in business, to solve problems or find new directions. I don't fall into any classic models of how to operate as a businessman. Instead of looking only for facts or logic, I'm constantly feeling my way through situations."

Unfortunately, most of us enter business believing that we can succeed on the strength of our education or job skills. As we progress, however, it's not uncommon for us to feel that more is required. Carol D., a highly creative advertising executive, learned that unless she followed her intuition, she ran into problem after problem:

> "I've learned to base my actions on my intuition, because, at around age thirty, I came to the conclusion that whenever I ignored my intuition and relied solely on what appeared to be logic, I made many mistakes. Now, when I act on my intuition, I'm always right . . . well, 90 percent of the time. I'm still not sure why I'm off from time to time, but that doesn't stop me from relying heavily on my gut feelings. The odds are better that way than on not heeding them. However, there still are times when inexplicably I resist my intuition."

As she talked, Carol gained insight into certain self-imposed limits she had placed on using her intuitive ability, which explained her decision to avoid using it at times. She saw that she allowed her intuition free rein only when she felt she was working within her area of expertise:

> "My job is to create, not to implement new advertising concepts. I use my intuition extensively to do this. I hold off using my intuition when it comes to implementing the concepts. Implementation is not my bag. I leave that up to others. As far as I'm concerned, my work is finished after the creative stage."

Carol also concluded that when charting unfamiliar work terri-
tory, she was unable to relax and use her intuitive abilities freely
and effectively:

> "In situations where I am confident and experienced,
> I'm committed to relying on my intuition. When I'm
> new to a situation and unsure of myself, I'm more like-
> ly to rely on logic. I'm beginning to realize, however,
> that my intuition is valid in any situation. I get in my
> own way when I become uncomfortable using it."

What about you? Do you believe in and value your intuition? If so, are you one of those people who talks about trusting your gut feelings, but when it comes right down to making
a decision that may affect your career or finances, ignores them
if logic points you in another direction? Or do you follow your
gut feelings only if you can enroll the support of other people?
If this describes you, or if you don't believe that you have intuitive abilities, it's time for a change that will enable you to take
charge of your business life. Alternatively, if you use your intuition only sporadically, it's time to expand this resource to its
full potential.

A Skill, Not a Mystical Experience

Intuition is not a paranormal "power" that only a chosen few are
lucky enough to be born with. Learning to use your intuition
effectively is like learning any other skill: It takes a receptive
mind, commitment, guidance, and practice. First, you must realize that this impressive gift is a natural, innate capability that
everyone possesses. It is blocked only by self-imposed, and limiting, beliefs and fears.

Because intuition, contrary to some people's belief, is part of
our innate human potential, you don't have to be in an altered or
mystical state of consciousness or undergo some outlandish
process to access it. Very simply, learning to use your intuitive
ability is comparable with learning a new language in school.
Electing to add this ability to your business arsenal could be an
important and beneficial decision that might change your business life substantially and permanently.

Understanding Your Intuition

To many of us, our intuitive process seems mysterious. It seemingly allows us to reach conclusions instantly without having access to all the facts we logically need and without the benefit of conscious reasoning. If you explore the intuitive side of your nature, you'll make two startling discoveries:

1. Much of what you think is intuitive, or what some people call sixth-sense, information, is really information coming from one or all of your five senses—sight, smell, touch, taste, and hearing.

2. In the process of strengthening your sixth-sense skills, you will strengthen your other five senses. Colors will appear brighter. You'll be more perceptive, seeing details with a new ease. Food will take on enhanced tastes and smells. And you'll be more sensitive to how things feel when touched. As this happens, your intellectual capabilities will improve. Your memory and recall will be better. You will think faster. And, finally, the process will bring you full circle. The more acute your five senses become, the greater your sixth-sense capacities will be. Intuitive information will flow effortlessly when you need it.

Your intuitive process works differently from your other sensing mechanisms. The actual working of your intuition occurs outside of your conscious awareness. You are aware of the input (the question or concern you are wrestling with) and you recognize the output (the answer to your concern), but you don't know what happens in between. In addition, the results of your intuitive efforts will present themselves in the form of one or more of a variety of mind or body awarenesses different for different people. They might, for example, surface indirectly, such as through symbolic dreams. Alternatively, they might present themselves more directly in the form of distinct spontaneous mental images, or as an inner voice telling you what you want to know or what you should do. Just as your mind and body signal when you are receiving answers from your intuition, they will similarly clue you in when you are blocking your intuitive process. You may experience coldness in your hands or negative thoughts. Quickly identifying when you're blocking the intuitive process is a key to developing your intuitive potential.

When faced with a decision, many intuitive businesspeople, instinctively and without being fully aware of what they are doing, mentally review their options to determine which one "feels" right, and when one does and is unclouded by fears, anxieties, or other destructive emotions, they know they have received an intuitive confirmation. Michael R., a successful entrepreneur and business visionary, explained his intuitive verification process this way:

> "I experience intuition as a sense of 'this is right,' and simultaneously I have a physical sensation in my stomach and chest. I don't understand how the process works, but when it does, I don't need any empirical evidence to back it up. In one recent meeting, an associate introduced the idea of establishing and running a trade association in our industry. I immediately had a feeling of opening up, that the idea was right, terrific in fact. I could feel it in my stomach and chest. At that moment, I felt relaxed and free."

The Perils of Actively Ignoring Your Intuition

You're always in touch with your intuitive knowing, but, if you're like most people, you may not realize it. The moment a question enters your mind, your intuition goes into gear, searching for answers. For a variety of reasons, which I will discuss later, you may block the free flow of your intuitive messages into your conscious awareness. And when these messages do get through, you might unknowingly ignore them or distort them by employing a variety of rationalizations, with the result that the information is of no value. As I began to work with my intuitive skills, I was constantly amazed at how often I rationalized away the results, to my detriment. I continued to take what people told me at face value, even when strong gut feelings told me differently. Recognizing how often you fail to acknowledge your intuitive messages, particularly those that surface in the elusive forms of symbolic dreams or vague physical sensations, is an important step in developing your full potential to think and act intuitively.

An international survey, conducted by Dr. Jagdish Parikh, former vice chairman of the World Business Academy, of 1,312 top senior managers from large industrial and service organizations in nine countries showed that managers were far more willing to use intuition in their personal life than in business. Raymond K., a senior sales executive for a furniture company, has the reverse problem; he chooses to go along with his intuition in business, but not in his personal life:

> "My intuition is involuntary. I can't block it, but I can ignore what it's telling me for my own reasons. I follow it implicitly in business, but my personal life is another matter. As an example, my first wife and I divorced when our kids were in their early teens. They would visit me, and, on the surface, it looked as though I were giving them enough of my time. My gut, however, told me that I needed to spend more time with them. I ignored these feelings because I was busy pursuing my own personal interests and my career. I regret doing this. My children had to make difficult adjustments because I wasn't there for them."

Focusing again on our performance in business, it is here, where we are continually challenged to manage people and situations, that we can most benefit from the input our intuition provides. But ironically, it is in this context that we often heed our intuition the least. For example, there may be times when you intuitively pick up information about yourself or your situation that makes you feel self-conscious and ill at ease. For instance, you may sense that your industry is about to take a downturn, or that a prospective customer feels your products are below par. Confronted with these insights, for many people the tendency is to unknowingly discount or distort the message to eliminate the discomfort.

Roberta G., an attorney, describes how she experiences this intuition block:

"I ignore my intuition when I don't like what it is telling me. In hindsight, I can look back on events and see how I used a variety of rationalizations to dismiss what it was telling me. I tell myself that my gut feelings can't be trusted without facts to back them up. I see now that this is a strategy to try to eliminate my own emotional discomfort. The result for me is lost growth opportunities."

If you don't like what your intuition is telling you, and you ignore it, you risk limiting your potential in business. Including your intuition among the tools you use to evaluate and manage yourself—and the people and situations that surround you—can help create the proper perspective with which to make decisions and base your actions. Seeing yourself and your situation clearly can be discomforting and challenge you to take risks like quitting a secure, but dead-end, job. In the long run, however, a significant portion of your success is contingent on your maintaining a clear perspective and actively changing what does not work.

—A Quiz—

Are You Ignoring Intuitive Messages?

How often do you overlook your intuitive signals? Here's a quick quiz to help you find out. A yes answer to any question below may be a clue that you're not taking full advantage of your inner sensing ability.

At times, do you, for reasons you cannot determine:

- Feel yourself getting uncomfortable or angry when in conversations with people?
- Feel instantly attracted or repelled by someone?
- Start to worry or get anxious?
- Begin to spontaneously think about someone?
- Go out of your way to make a stranger feel at ease?

There is a reason for everything you feel, think, and do. When you're not consciously aware of why you are responding in a particular way, consider the possibility that your own unconscious intuitive feedback is influencing your thoughts, feelings, and actions.

A Woman's Edge—That Men Can Acquire

Generally, women have an advantage over men in developing intuitive skills for business. From childhood, men are encouraged to control their feelings, to be stoic in the face of problems. In effect, men are taught to root their thoughts and actions predominantly in fact and logic. Our intuitive process, however, demands that we be unrestrained by rules and pure logic. It requires us to mentally let go of our conscious thoughts and attitudes about people, situations, and events, and instead allow our inner sensing capacity to take over so that more visceral reactions can surface into our consciousness.

Even more difficult for many men to overcome is the common attitude that intuition is part of a woman's nature, which might suggest that it is something that "real" men don't, or shouldn't, have. As a result, many men actually repress their feeling or sensing nature. An initial hurdle for them, then, is to understand that intuition is a universal human trait, and to embrace their feeling or sensing nature, dismissing any thoughts that doing so reflects poorly on their manhood.

Although, generally speaking, women have an edge in developing their intuitive skills fully, using these same skills can create challenges in today's business environment. The business world has traditionally been a male-dominated club. Men have set the rules of play, and the rules state that feelings have no place in business. In order to succeed in this environment, women frequently feel pressured to conform to the behavior that the men around them display. Feeling intimidated, they sometimes allow the spontaneity that must be present if they are to connect with their intuition to give way to unduly restrained consideration. As a result, some women hold back expressing intuitive ideas to avoid the risk of having them summarily discounted, or ridiculed.

Jane R., a former insurance company executive and now a very successful entrepreneur and human potential consultant, recalls her inability to effectively use her intuition in business this way:

> "When I worked in corporate America, I felt pressured to suppress my intuitive thoughts. They often weren't trusted or rewarded by my superiors. Every idea had to be backed up with data. You had to be able to point to something solid—a prior success, research, or years of experience. Now, as a business owner, I can use my intuition freely. I have no one to answer to but myself. Results that work are all that matter."

Jane's experience was particularly confusing because on occasion her intuitive ideas were welcome, and on other occasions she was openly criticized by her co-workers or bosses.

> "There were days from time to time when I was rewarded for being intuitive and spontaneous, and other days when I was specifically told to put a lid on my flow of ideas. Invariably, on the days when I was told to ratchet it down, it was clear that my ideas were making others uncomfortable—either because they felt inadequate for not being able to offer suggestions, or because my style irritated or threatened them."

What happens to many highly motivated women in this environment? They emotionally and intuitively shut down, something that impedes their progress and erodes their confidence. Jane was lucky; she got through her career crisis by quitting and starting her own business. The experience, however, took an emotional toll:

> "I was so confused by being told to put a lid on my spontaneous suggestions that, when I left to go out on my own, I didn't know who I was or what my real

skills were. I talked to a lot of people, hoping they could give me some insights about what they thought I could do. I wound up starting a business to help people like myself, people looking for career direction and validation of their worth. When clients come to me, they are often feeling battered and fragile, unsure—as I was—of who they are. A great deal of my early work with them is intuitively 'reading' them, listening between the lines to assess their abilities and start them on the right course. I call this process 'the touchey feelies,' and clients are consistently amazed that I can describe who they are so quickly and accurately."

So what's the answer for both men and women? It's very simple. Both must acknowledge their feeling and sensing nature in business, and not be intimidated by those who are frightened by, or resentful of, these human aspects.

A Side Benefit—Personal Growth

In addition to supplying a business advantage, developing and using your intuition will also bring personal growth. Without your being aware of it, barriers that could block your satisfaction and progress in business and in life will drop away. You'll see all people in a more positive and accepting way. You'll view yourself in a less judgmental manner. The business process will come under your control. And with all of this comes increased maturity.

Conclusion

There is no doubt that in today's ever-changing and demanding business environment, you must not overlook developing any skill that can increase your chances of survival or success. While intuition is not taught at business school or accepted as a mainstream strategy for solving business challenges, we have seen that it is an innate and effective ability that many businesspeople have developed and honed to help them assess sit-

uations and people, make decisions, or select business directions. Although women are culturally more open to tapping
their intuition than men, both sexes face challenges in engaging
their intuition in the business world. Doing so, however, is
important in helping them become well-rounded individuals
who are able to maintain and operate from the benefit of a clear
perspective. Personal growth, clarity, and informed reasoning
are just a few of the rewards that spring from integrating our
intuitive nature in business. In the next chapter, we explore
how to develop the mindset necessary to allow your intuitive
potential to be realized.

Chapter 2

Breaking Through

"If you can dream it, you can do it"
—Walt Disney

Developing your intuition is not a traditional learning experience, but more a process of becoming aware of and using an innate ability and applying it in a business context. This is not difficult, but it does require you to let go of old patterns of thinking, as well as illusions about yourself and others, life, and business, that up until now may have been comforting, but that get in the way of predictable business progress.

Once you initiate this process of clearing or letting go, much of the development will occur below the level of your conscious awareness, where the subconscious mind can work out the intricate details of freeing your intuition. So, expect moments when you feel you are making no progress. If you are committed to building your intuitive talent, you can expect dramatic breakthroughs from time to time.

You'll discover that you cannot power your way to developing your inner gifts by using your analytical ability. Rather, you must learn to clear blocks to intuition so that intuitive information can flow freely. Those of you who have been called upon to solve a complex business problem creatively know that attempting to force an answer rarely works. The best approach is to get a clear picture of the problem in your mind, and then forget about it. When you least expect it, possibly when you're driving home from work or taking a shower, an answer will surface in your thoughts.

You may have to break the thinking patterns of a lifetime that tempt you to understand and trust only things based on your life experiences, what you or someone else can scientifically prove, or book knowledge. Be prepared instead to accept insights that you won't be able to validate in a traditional way. It never ceases to amaze me that people who sit in judgment on the limits of human potential often do so based on what their life experience has been, or on mainstream, traditional thinking. Remember, when you're trying to evaluate something you've never experienced and you base your evaluation on past experience and knowledge, you limit yourself.

Learn to welcome your intuitive messages. You'll come to know that not a day goes by when, for a variety of reasons, you actively fail to recognize, and take full advantage of, your incredible sixth-sense potential. So, relax and explore. Don't be afraid to test your limits. Have some fun. You won't be disappointed. And you might even be astonished.

In order to fully develop your intuitive potential, both a belief that success is possible and a relaxed attitude are essential. This chapter will show you how to accomplish both.

How to Approach Using Your Intuition for Business

The best way to use your intuitive abilities when confronted with a business problem or concern is to begin by gathering as much information as possible in a traditional way. The more information you take in through your five senses, the more effective you will be in applying your intuitive skills and creating an amalgam of intuited possibilities and practical considerations to reach the best possible conclusion. The mistake many people make is trying to use their intuition before becoming fully informed. Keep in mind that your intuition is an adjunct, not an alternative, to your other senses.

So, when confronted with a business problem, seek the advice of everyone you know who may be of help. If your challenge is to improve manufacturing operations, visit the plant floor and take in every aspect of the operation. Listen to the sounds. Take the time to sense the flow of work. If you're involved in designing a product, get hold of a piece of the material it is to be made from. Run your hand over it to see how it feels. As you're doing this, relax and close your eyes, and see what thoughts come into your mind. Pay attention to any sensations you experience. If you're about to write a business plan, look at what others have written. If solid and meaningful seminars are available, take full advantage of them. Don't try to reach any conclusion until you've examined every possible detail, even ones you don't think are relevant. Very simply, learn to use your five sense capabilities to their fullest to gather information, and then turn your intuition on.

Chip T., a product research developer, describes his intuitive workings as follows:

> "I think intuitive answers happen as a result of an accumulation of facts that come together, which is then the basis for making the best possible business decision. It seems to be an instinctual reaction to the totality of information and events, rather than something you've arrived at in a logical manner."

Making an Intuition Breakthrough

Choosing to release your intuitive skill is up to you. There is no magic formula. But there are four keys. You must:

1. Focus on your intuitive possibilities.
2. Allow yourself to dream about these possibilities, as you did when you were a child.
3. Be willing to set goals for yourself that you never thought were possible—to stretch your emotional comfort zone.
4. Expect that you can achieve these goals regardless of what other people say.

All this requires that you overcome any inner limiting beliefs about your intuitive possibilities. Remember, everyone is intuitive. And virtually everyone discounts, ignores, or dismisses the full use of his or her intuitive abilities on the basis of beliefs other people force on him or her. We fail in life when we accept limits imposed by others.

Check Your Intuition Attitude

Let's begin your breakthrough process by checking your intuition attitude. Do you qualify any success you might have in developing your intuition with any of the following thoughts?

- I hope it is possible to develop my intuitive capabilities.
- The thought of having an intuitive capability is exciting, but I'll have to wait and see if it's really possible.
- I will do my best to develop my intuition.
- I doubt that I can develop my intuition, but I'll remain open to the possibility.
- My spouse (or friend or associate) thinks it's an absurd pursuit.
- I hope I uncover only positive information.
- What good would it do to have intuitive abilities? Business success is never in my control.
- I have mixed feelings about the results of accessing my intuition.

If the answer to any of these is yes, or if you harbor any similar limiting beliefs about intuition, or specifically about your intuitive ability, you need to reprogram yourself for breakthrough success. And that means rescripting your beliefs about intuition to eliminate all inner resistance so that connecting with your intuitive source becomes second nature, requiring nothing more than an initiating thought.

Program Your Mind for Success

Peak-performance experts have shown that you cannot achieve solid success in anything you go after unless you believe that you can reach your goal—totally and without question. Denis Waitly, a developmental psychologist and the former chairman of psychology of the U.S. Olympic Committee's Council of Medicine, as well as other human potential experts, has consistently shown that we are limited largely by our own beliefs. In his best-selling cassette tape series *The Psychology of Winning*

(Nightingale Conant Corporation), Waitly concludes that we are what we think. He says that the limits of our human potential are based upon unfounded beliefs imposed on us by other people, directly or indirectly, and not upon reality, and that if you aim for success, you will achieve, but possibly not always on your timetable.

Some of your limiting beliefs can be eliminated simply by your recognizing them. Unfortunately, many others, such as any disbelief about your intuitive potential, take more effort. These are the ones that are so deeply embedded in your subconscious that eliminating them may be possible only through a continual, conscious, and concentrated commitment to reprogramming your thinking—the type of reprogramming that record-breaking athletes and highly successful salespeople are taught. This begins with rescripting your belief system by establishing for yourself firm goals that you can become passionate about achieving. Can you, right now, call to mind something that you have dreamed of achieving in business, but which you have not set a firm goal for and actively pursued because you believe it to be beyond your reach? If so, it's time to take control over your career.

Surprisingly, active and consistent goal setting is not something many people are accustomed to doing. As a result, their chances of success in anything are typically the same as their chances of winning a state lottery—very small. Successful businesspeople, however, do set goals, and consciously move toward them daily. Achieving major breakthroughs in accessing your intuition is no different. Goal setting can make the difference between success and failure. In developing your intuitive skill, first you must decide unequivocally that you are going to do it. And then, keeping this objective firmly fixed in your mind, you must enthusiastically believe that you can.

A fascinating example of the value and power of goal setting is a study of the Yale class of 1973. Immediately before graduation, the seniors were asked if they had set personal and business goals for themselves. Only approximately 2 percent said that they had. In 1993, the class was again polled to see what its members had accomplished over the twenty-year period. Amazingly, it was found that the majority of the wealth of the class as a group resided in the 2 percent of the class who had set goals for themselves. Clearly, goal setting works.

Effective Goal Setting

Peak-performance athletes and other successful people have been using goal-setting techniques for many years. Golfers, for example, have improved their golf game, in part, by visualizing themselves over and over making a perfect swing. The techniques they use are straightforward. You can adopt them too by:

- Learning whatever skills are necessary to achieve your goal
- Mentally envisioning the details of having achieved the goal
- Believing that success is possible—without qualification
- Eliminating all negative thoughts about your goal
- Expecting success to happen
- Never losing sight of your goal
- Making every effort necessary to reach your goal
- Being patient
- Using obstacles to make necessary course corrections

Here's how you can apply these general principles to developing your intuitive skill:

—A Technique—

Setting and Reaching Your Intuition Development Goal

The journey to developing your intuition begins with believing that your success is not only possible but inevitable.

Make an unqalified commitment to fully develop your intuition for business.

1. Generally remind yourself of this goal each day until you have achieved it. As soon as you wake up in the morning and once again in the evening before you go to bed, say, for example, "I am dedicated to developing to the fullest my innate intuitive ability."

2. Mentally envision yourself using your intuition effectively at least once each business day. For example, before a business presentation, mentally picture yourself intuiting issues that may surface in your audience's mind, and then intelligently incorporating them into your presentation.
3. Confidently expect that you will develop and successfully use your intuition in business.
4. Refuse to indulge any doubts about your success, or any negative thinking about your natural intuitive ability.
5. Each day make an effort to use your intuition in some business situation at least once. Try to intuit the agenda of a colleague whose motivations you cannot fully understand.
6. When you're incorrect about something you have tried to intuit, make every effort to determine why you were wrong, using the principles and suggestions in this book.

Envision Your Intuition Goal

To understand how visualizing yourself acting intuitively works, consider the functioning of your conscious and subconscious mind. Your conscious mind is responsible for taking in—perceiving—information. It then reaches a conclusion or decision based upon what has been perceived. Once made, the decision is sent to your subconscious mind, the part of your brain that, in effect, takes control and facilitates the carrying out of your conscious decisions. Assume that you want to get up and walk to the copier machine. You don't need to think to yourself, "Okay, get up, turn, left foot, right foot." Once you've made the decision, your unconscious mind gets you moving where you want to go. In a similar manner, when your conscious goal is to develop your intuition, a message is sent to your subconscious, which immediately begins the implementation process. All you have to do is let it happen.

In going after a goal, when you incorporate a clear mental picture of what you want to achieve—envisioning yourself, for example, in business situations where you are successfully using your intuition—and repeat this over and over, you can accelerate your ability to acquire the intuitive ability that is your intuition goal.

—A Technique—
Envisioning Yourself as Intuitive

You want to be able to trust your gut in business. Here's how to use envisioning to speed up the process.

1. Assume that you must make an important computer sales presentation to a prospective customer whom you have never been able to sell before. On the sales call, you want to use your intuition to determine what the problem could be.

2. Mentally see yourself making your sales presentation in a meeting with your prospective customer, putting in as many details as possible. For example, visualize:

   ■ The clothes you will be wearing
   ■ How your hair will be combed
   ■ What his or her office looks like
   ■ What your customer looks like, including the clothes he or she may be wearing—even if you have to guess

3. Go over in your mind the details of your conversation, such as:

   ■ Every word you plan to say
   ■ Objections your customer has raised in the past, or may raise at this presentation

4. Now see yourself intuiting ways to overcome your customer's objections, and then successfully persuading him or her to make the purchase. If you imagine your customer saying that there is no room in the budget to make a purchase, allow your thoughts to roam freely to see if you can

sense and seize upon a possible solution. (If you have trouble coming up with a solution, imagine yourself asking the customer what you must do to overcome the problem or counter the objection.)

5. Finally, envision yourself successfully persuading your customer to buy the computer. Fill in the details of the conclusion of your successful meeting, such as:

   ■ Your order form being signed
   ■ The product order resting in your hands.
   ■ The product being delivered, set up, and operating at his or her company's location

The more details you use, the clearer the visualization will be. Do this exercise for five minutes at least twice a day, at a time when you will not be disturbed, starting, if possible, one week before the situation in which you plan to use your intuition.

Engage Your Imagination

Imagination is responsible for all of life's incredible breakthroughs. Inventors, artists, singers, actors, and successful businesspeople can attest to this fact. Thomas Edison, the great American inventor, had over 1,000 patents—all sparked by his imagination.

Your imagination is a key to unlocking your intuitive potential. This may seem suspect to you at first. You may think that engaging your imagination will lead you astray—that what surfaces will be pure fantasy. But, as you experiment with connecting with your intuition, you'll see that this will not be the case.

By engaging your imagination, you escape the controls or delusions of your analytical, or robot, mind. You are able to be creative, glimpsing ways of looking at people and situations that have hitherto escaped you. In engaging your imagination, you become optimistic and enjoy a sense of freedom. In turn, this creates a state of mind that paves the way for your intuitive messages to surface into your conscious awareness.

Abraham Maslow, a preeminent American psychologist, scratched the surface of the power that comes from being in the right frame of mind. He found that by inducing positive mental states, people were able to do incredible things. Those who are unable to put themselves in a positive, or receptive, frame of mind become mental robots, following the unimaginative roads laid out by other people who had accomplished little, if anything, of real value in life.

You cannot force the working of your intuitive sensing mechanism. As a result, working with your intuition may be challenging simply because getting results will depend on your ability to act in direct opposition to the way you've acted all your life and to go against a belief indoctrinated in childhood—that if you want something, you must work, and work hard, to achieve it. The opposite holds true when releasing your innate intuitive ability. It takes effort to prevent your intuitive messages from naturally surfacing.

The Need for Courage

Learning to trust your intuition requires courage. More often than not, determining the outcome of your intuitive business choices takes time. Typically, there will be no benchmarks along the way against which to measure if you're on the right track, and there will be no support from business associates. So, in the beginning, expect a sleepless night or two. But if you persist, and have faith, you will gain the confidence you need.

Soon after he took over the management of a financial services firm in New York City, Peter W. had a period of self-doubt about using his intuition in business. But he also had faith in his gut feelings, a faith that ultimately enabled him to move ahead of his competition and build his company into a large, thriving, international firm. Here's how Peter W. described his early experience:

"When I was thirty-seven and made head of my company, there were twenty or so partners, five in their fifties and sixties, two in their late forties, and the rest in their early thirties to mid-forties. The oldest partners were the rainmakers, so when they retired, there would be no one bringing in business. I thought about this and set up an informal sales and marketing program. My gut told me that bankers were a group of people who could refer business to us. I positioned our company as a good middle-market accounting firm—not as big as the Big Eight, and not as small as a local firm. I told my partners to go down to Wall Street and start knocking on doors. The older partners said it wouldn't work, and the younger ones didn't want to do it. I persisted and persuaded everyone to go along with my idea. Using this strategy, the first year we brought in about $100,000, and by the end of five years, the program was bringing in over $1.5 million annually. Even though everyone around me was initially reluctant to work the program, my intuition told me it was right."

Potential Sources of Intuitive Information

What we're taught to believe as children—to rely only on information that is verifiable in a traditional way—often gets in the way of our progress when developing intuition. If you're stuck with this belief, it may be helpful to compare the working of your intuitive process with the creative process of an abstract artist. The abstract artist acts as a medium between the brush and her or his creativity. The artist simply begins painting, and the images flow. He or she gives no thought to where the images originate, all that matters is getting an evocative result. It would be ridiculous for an artist to hold off the creative process until he or she knew the source of his or her creative ideas. Well, the same is true in developing your intuitive capabilities. Like the artist, all you have to do is allow the process to happen, and then engage your reasoning to measure the results.

Peter T., a marketing executive, expressed the typical attitude many businesspeople have about using their intuition this way:

> "I accept intuition as a part of my innate nature, but when making business decisions, I don't easily rely on it, especially if I think I can get hard data to support my decision. The more important the decision, the less comfortable I am trusting my intuition, because I don't know how this information comes into my head."

Peter's analytical inclinations get in the way of developing his intuitive gift. Although he acknowledges his intuitive capability, he is uncomfortable unless he understands all the analytical links to a decision or conclusion. And the less Peter uses his intuition, the less it will be available to him.

When you think about it, does it matter where your sixth-sense information comes from? Obviously, it doesn't, as long as the information is accurate. Unfortunately, unless they know its source, and the source fits with their beliefs about what is humanly possible, some people are uncomfortable relying on it. What about you? If, for example, an employee told you that she could intuitively read people very well and, as a result, knew that your business partner was cheating you, would you believe it? Possibly?

Let's briefly consider some potential sources of intuitive information. The following list of possible sources of your intuitive information is compiled from various ideas that parapsychologists and other scientific researchers and scientists investigating intuition have proposed. They are not based on scientific proof, which is, of course, difficult to apply to matters of intuition. Just use this list to help open your mind to the variety of places that intuition may have its source. It might be interesting to make a mental note of your immediate reaction to each suggestion. After you've worked with your intuition for a period of time, review these suggestions again and see if you feel differently. You might be surprised.

Possible Sources of Intuitive Information

Consider that your intuitive messages may come from one or more of a variety of sources, such as:

- Accessing what noted psychiatrist Carl Jung referred to as the collective unconscious
- An unconscious amalgam of your five-sense information
- Information from one or more of your five senses that you're uncomfortable acknowledging directly
- Tapping into other people's thoughts or emotions
- Telepathic messages from others
- Vibratory information stored in inanimate objects, such as someone's watch
- Seeing the past and future simultaneously
- Tapping into a source of ancient knowledge universally available to everyone
- A higher power

Can you think of any other possible sources of intuitive information? If so, write them down for future reference, even if you think they're ridiculous. Reconsider them as you hone your intuition.

Accept What You May Learn

Have you ever walked away from a business meeting worrying about the impression you've made, or been concerned about whether or not your boss or co-workers thought well of you? Most of us have, and if we sense that the answer is not favorable, it's not unusual for us to repress or discount these feelings in an effort to eliminate our anxieties. However, seeing the truth is the solution to every progress block. Knowing that your boss dislikes you can be stressful, but it can also provide the incentive to change what he or she doesn't like or, if it's a compatibility problem, to look for a new job to avoid a career roadblock.

To use your full intuitive potential, you must be willing to face things about yourself or someone else, or about a situation in business, as they are, no matter what they may be. If you run away from the prospect of experiencing momentary discomfort by attempting to repress what you may feel because it is something you don't want to know, you will inhibit your intuitive message flow, as well as your potential for progress in business.

Mari T., a top-notch executive secretary, frequently experienced intuitive messages, which, at times, presented her with insights that she preferred not to be aware of. She decided to allow only what she considered good messages to come through. This was a mistake for her in business:

> "When I was younger, I often experienced intuitive feelings. I tried to verify these feelings, and soon learned how accurate they were. It was an exciting time. As I paid more attention to these feelings, my intuitive ability expanded. I became good at quickly sizing up people and situations. Unfortunately, I also sensed things about people that hurt my feelings or were very upsetting. The older I got, the more difficulty I had in accepting what I considered negative information that created conflict for me. With some effort, I've learned to block uncomfortable information, allowing only good intuitive messages to come through."

Mari's effort to manage her sixth-sense flow has limited her feelings of personal discomfort, but has also hampered her full use of her intuition for business. She is currently working in a job that she does not like, and one that does not allow her to use her full potential. And she has fallen victim to the type of lack-of-success rationalization that the world of business accepts as solid reasoning:

> "I don't have a college education, and I'm middle-aged. These are the things that really hold me back from getting promotions and more business responsibilities."

It is highly possible that if Mari hadn't tried to manage her intuitive messages, and had been willing to accept the good with what she perceived as the bad, she would be pursuing a business direction she would find fulfilling. This became evident in our discussions. She often referred to a happy and successful business endeavor that clearly did not depend on education or age, and one in which she had used her talents to their fullest.

> "A number of years ago, I was working as an executive assistant when my husband started a food catering business. I gave up a good job because my gut told me to go work with him, that it would be the right decision. Everything about that venture went well. The business was profitable, and I loved the work, and meeting people. I used my intuition freely in the business to, for example, quickly establish a rapport with a prospective customer. I've never been so satisfied in business."

Unfortunately for Mari, the catering business was sold, and she promptly returned to a mundane work environment, one in which she relies less on her intuition.

—A Quick Test—
Do You Resist Your Intuition?

Many people actively resist their intuitive process, adopting ways of working or thinking that create barriers to their awareness of intuitive messages. If any of the following is true, you too may be doing this and thereby limiting your potential. In business, do you:

- Avoid doing things that feel right, unless you have the support of someone else?
- Feel uncomfortable working by yourself?

- Think lack of education or job experience or your age holds you back?
- Feel that you are generally unlucky?
- Give other people advice based on your intuition, but don't follow it yourself?
- Overanalyze or reject creative business initiatives that pop into your mind?
- Have recurring negative thoughts?
- Have trouble paying attention during meetings?
- Have moments of sudden exhaustion?
- Hold back sharing your ideas?

At this stage, don't be concerned about why any of these occurrences, or others that are similar, could show that you are resisting your intuition. It is more important to become aware of thoughts, inclinations, and situations that may directly result from your unknowingly resisting your intuitive messages.

The Logical Thinking Dilemma

By logically and systematically linking our position with hard facts that can't be faulted, it's easy to persuade people to accept our conclusions. Businesspeople who effectively use logic gain power, out-negotiate others, and reap financial rewards. On the other hand, intuitive positions may not be persuasive because businesspeople generally demand factual support, and sometimes it is simply not available. The irony is that intuitive solutions are often the ones responsible for major business breakthroughs. Although logic is essential in the business process, it can lead you astray when it is not integrated with intuition because it is typically based on past experiences and conceptions that need to be recharacterized if progress is to be made in a current situation. And placing too much emphasis on these past experiences can block your intuitive process.

Mackie T., a market research manager, discussed her dependence on logic:

"I am habitually analytical. Analysis is what makes sense to me. I fall into the trap of believing that other people are as logical as I am. Yet, all around me, I see many people making good decisions that aren't based upon logic. I appreciate their courage and faith, but I'm not able to do it myself. I think this has been an impediment to my business progress."

Our struggle to keep logic in a proper perspective may, in part, be due to our human makeup. Neuroscientists believe that the portion of our brain that processes information logically, the left brain, is generally dominant. Consequently, the part of our brain that functions intuitively, the right brain, may take a back seat in our approaches to business. The right brain is known to look at things globally, whereas the left brain processes information one piece at a time. So, although it's believed that both left- and right-brain functions are always occurring, if we are too intent on left-brain analysis, we can inadvertently block the intuitive contribution of our right brain.

A wonderful story related to me recently by Peter T., a marketing executive and avid golfer, demonstrates how analysis can cause intuition paralysis. Peter has spent years trying to improve his golf game. He analyzed every aspect, including the mechanics of the swing and the selection of the most appropriate club. However, it was only when he turned the job over to his intuition that he made real progress:

"I'm an avid golfer. I believe that golf, played correctly, is a highly intuitive game. Sports psychologists write a lot about reaching a specific zone of awareness, where you can allow your intuition to take over when you're playing. When you're in that zone, it feels like you're suspended in time. There are no thoughts or distractions. It's a heightened state of consciousness. Great golfers can get into this zone and stay there for all eighteen holes. I've managed to achieve it for three or four holes at a time. It's a great feeling. You are totally in the moment—not thinking about the last shot, and not analyzing the next one. You visualize where the ball is going to go, and it goes there."

I asked Peter how he creates this state of mind for himself, and his answer was interesting:

> "My golf coach encouraged me to get into a repetitive movement routine. He suggested that before putting, I make twenty little gestures—tugging my pants, or handling the club in a certain way—and make the same repetitive gestures every time I'm about to putt. The repetitive rhythm process apparently makes its easy for intuition to take over."

Even with this success, Peter is still reluctant to tap into his intuition for business:

> "I guess you could follow this logic and apply the same theory to business. You know, get into a zone where your intuition takes over and leads you, and then find logical support for it. I'm afraid to try, because I know my management would frown on this type of approach."

In some companies, Peter's approach may be the safest. Business is often preoccupied with analysis. Fortunately, this is beginning to change. New economic demands on business are pushing managers to consider other approaches to solving problems, and to embrace a bottom-up, team-oriented management style rather than one that is top-down. Multiculturalism, the blending of professionals with differing operating styles, and greater collegiality rather than old-fashioned paternalism are combining to create an ambiguous and richly textured workplace. Intuitive types are found to thrive here. A by-product of their intuition is often a talent for understanding others and working with them to foster team spirit. They also demonstrate an ability to divine creative strategies amid the clutter and information overload of a fast-forward business environment where many of the old analytical approaches that were rooted in time-consuming fact finding fail to produce the necessary results.

Body/Mind Signals

You'll notice that when you're connected with your intuitive channel, you will experience a distinct mind state and body sensation that will be uniquely recognizable, and that will begin just before information flow and will last throughout the intuitive connection. At this time, you'll feel physically relaxed and mentally at ease, almost as though your mind is in neutral. As soon as your intuitive connection ends, whether because all necessary information has been conveyed or because your inner resistance has shut it down, the mind and body experience also ends. If you find that you're vacillating in and out of the mind state and body feeling as messages surface, this is your signal that you are consciously or unconsciously blocking or distorting your intuitive information flow. If this occurs, take a break and reengage your intuitive efforts at a later time. Information received during such a mind and body vacillation is not reliable.

Using an Intuition Bridge

An easy way to facilitate a connection with your intuitive source is to use what I will call an intuition bridge, something that helps you to relax and shift your focus inward and away from your life preoccupations and other intuition distractions.

You can use as an intuition bridge a simple object, such as a bowl of water or a clear glass paperweight. You can also use a piece of jewelry or object of clothing belonging to a person you're trying to intuitively connect with, or a photograph of that person. Or you could use a smooth, round stone, a candle, or, believe it or not, a crystal ball—anything that you're comfortable with, and that will gently bring your focus inward.

An intuition bridge could be an aspect of the environment you inhabit while you're engaging your intuitive process—soft background music, particularly music that slows the heart rate and produces a relaxed state. Some suggestions for you to consider are Mozart's *Vesperae Solemnes de Confessore*, Handel's "Largo" (from *Xerxes*), Dvorak's "Largo" (from Symphony no. 9), and Paul Horn's *Inside the Taj Mahal*. Experiment with your music choices. And use your intuition to guide you in selecting what is most appropriate for you. If you find that music creates too much of a distraction, experiment with the room lighting: dim it or use soft colored lights, such as blue or pink. Again, use your intuition to guide you in your selection.

Here's an exercise to show you how to use an intuition bridge.

—A Technique—
Connecting Using an Intuition Bridge

In this exercise, you'll learn how to work with an intuition bridge to facilitate your intuition connection. Approach this exercise playfully. There is no right or wrong way to do it. Just relax and experiment, without any expectations. As you do the exercise, use your imagination. Let go of any need to have a defined result. Think of it as a quick vacation—a jaunt for the mind. And don't judge anything—yourself, your thoughts, your abilities, or the inner suggestions that you receive.

1. Set aside some time for yourself in the next day or so, preferably in the evening, when you are not tired and you can be alone and undisturbed for at least twenty minutes. Use as your intuition bridge for this journey a small bowl of water, six to ten inches in diameter. Pick a simple bowl that you find aesthetically appealing. Fill it with clear, cold water, and place it on a table in front of where you will sit. When you're ready, sit down in front of the bowl, preferably in a straight-backed chair. The bowl should be approximately two feet away from your body. It might be helpful to record the following instructions on an audio cassette, so that you can follow them without the effort or interruption needed for reading.

2. Focus a relaxed gaze on the water in the bowl, and keep it there as you let go of your concerns. Let your mind quiet down. Relax. Give yourself whatever time is necessary to clear your mind of all thought static. Keep your eyes gently focused on the water. If your gaze drifts away, gently

return it to the bowl. Don't try to remain intensely focused on the bowl. Take as long as you wish with this part of the journey. If you've placed these instructions on an audio cassette, leave about five minutes of quiet time here before you begin the next instruction.

3. When you're ready, think about someone not in your presence for five minutes. Say to yourself the following:
"I wonder what [*name of person*] is doing at the moment." Do nothing more. Make no effort to pull up memories. Just sit and gaze casually at the water in the bowl. Let events flow in your mind without any expectations. Don't force yourself to look at the bowl. However, every time you become consciously aware that you're looking elsewhere, return your gaze to the water. If you feel inclined to close your eyes, do so. Leave them closed for as long as is comfortable. There are no fixed rules on this journey.

4. Now, for the next ten minutes, picture in your mind where this person might be right now, such as on a business trip or in a car, and what this person might be doing. When you have a sense of what the person might be doing, ask him or her a question, any question that comes to your mind. Wait for an answer. If the person seems willing to talk to you, carry on a conversation. Talk about anything you feel like discussing. Ask the person about his or her childhood, or about his or her hopes and dreams. If you find anxious thoughts about unrelated matters, such as pressures of work or home, creeping into your mind, don't resist them. As soon as comfortably possible, however, gently return your thoughts to your subject.

As you picture the person in your mind's eye, see if you can spot anything unusual. Is the person wearing something unusual? Look for anything in his or her surroundings that seems out of place. Your intuition may be conveying information to you symbolically. See if you can guess at the meaning of this apparent symbol.

Are you having any pounding or unusual thoughts? Do you hear any sounds, such as a musical note or a melody? Explore any gut feelings that you have, or any other physical sensations. Take a guess at what they could mean.

Do you have any sudden knowing about the person or anything else, such as an unrelated event? Let your thoughts float anywhere they choose—even to other people or other situations.

5. Bring your journey to a conclusion when you feel ready to do so, or when you've found yourself back in your regular state of awareness.

Releasing your intuition is a dynamic process. For your intuition to grow, it must evolve and change. Trust what happens. The point of the preceding exercise is not to fulfill any expectation, but to learn to allow your imagination to actively engage. Do the exercise as often as you can, focusing in on different people or situations. The more you practice, the easier it will be to connect with your intuitive source on demand. Your ultimate objective is to be able to connect with your intuition without the use of an intuition bridge—for accessing your intuitive source to become second nature, something that automatically occurs anytime you have a question about something or someone.

Kick-Starting Your Intuitive Ability

You can kick-start your intuitive ability by beginning to use it daily, whether or not you're confident in doing so. A helpful way to look at the process of developing your intuitive skills is to compare it with learning to ride a bicycle. You're born with the innate ability to ride a bicycle, but you have to learn how to become comfortable performing this exercise—balancing, pedaling, and stopping. Through trial and error, you become skilled at riding. The actual intricacies of the riding process, such as the mechanics of balancing, occur outside of your conscious awareness. Learning to use, and actively using, your intuition is no different. It is a natural latent ability. And it's available when you have the desire to develop it. And, as with riding a bike, you have to go through a trial-and-error period to hone the skill. The more you use your intuition, the easier it becomes. There is one final thought you should keep in mind about developing your intuitive skill: If you allow it to, your intuition will actually guide you in its development.

Conclusion

To release your innate intuitive ability, you must eliminate any limiting beliefs about what you think is possible. Programming yourself for ultimate success and seeing as your goal the development of your intuition for use in business is important to your progress. You can expect your desire to respond intuitively to often collide with an ingrained tendency to use only logic in making assessments. But both your mind and your body will provide clues to help you recognize when you are successfully engaging or blocking your intuition. Particularly in the initial stages of learning to access your intuition, you may find it helpful to use an intuition bridge, something that will help you let go of any preoccupations or distractions that block or distort your intuitive messages and access to your inner guide.

Chapter 3

What to Expect as You Release Your Intuitive Potential

"I have mixed feelings about following my intuition,
even though I know it's always best for me to do so."
—Peter R.,
physician, businessman

As you start to release your full intuitive potential, you may experience new awarenesses about yourself and the world around you. In any new endeavor, knowing what to expect is comforting. In this chapter you'll learn about what you may experience as you develop your intuitive ability. Use this information as a guidepost to keep yourself on the right track and moving forward.

Pushing the Limits of Your Emotional Comfort Zone

Most people resist change, even when it's for the better. They prefer to stick with what they know, although it may be less than satisfactory. To avoid putting themselves into business situations that may take them out of their emotional comfort zone, they make compromises that they know could hold them back, and then invent great rationalizations to justify their position. For example, speaking at a department meeting or business outing can be good for a business career, but it is something many people find emotionally uncomfortable and look for any excuse to avoid doing.

When you choose to remain in your emotional comfort zone, adventure takes a back seat. You wait for someone else to pave the way and tell you what to do, and assure you that the path is safe. Exploring your intuitive capabilities is an adventure into the unknown. Don't be surprised if you find some natural inner resistance on the way. Success is dependent on your willingness to stretch your emotional limits.

My favorite story of people waiting for others to tell them what's possible concerns an Englishman, Roger Bannister, the first athlete to run the measured mile in under four minutes. For hundreds of years prior to Bannister's record-breaking accomplishment on May 6, 1954, running a mile in under four minutes was thought to be physiologically impossible. However, no sooner had the word of Bannister's triumph spread around the world than other runners matched Bannister's barrier-breaking run. Following Bannister, in 1954, thirty-seven other runners ran the mile in under four minutes, and, even more amazing, in 1955, over 300 athletes broke the four-minute-mile barrier. Bannister proved that it was possible, eliminating self-imposed blocks that other runners had accepted.

Signs of Denial

Developing your intuitive potential may require that you push the limits of what is considered conventional business methodology and thinking. This may bring you to the edge of your emotional comfort zone, where thoughts, feelings, and sensations that will make you want to give up may occur, tempting you to believe that you're on the wrong track, or that what you're pursuing is not possible.

View these denials as signals that you are blocking your progress. Be on the look out for self-doubts, including the following:

- Where's the real proof for what I'm doing?
- Even if I develop my intuition, I still won't attain my goals.

- This is a waste of time.
- How can I be sure this will help me?
- I can't possibly learn to do this.
- The experts say this is impossible.

Mixed Feelings

Even if you are initially excited about the possibilities of intuition building, you may have mixed feelings once you consider the ramifications. You could become reluctant to experience unsettling insights, or to acknowledge that others, in turn, may have insights about you and the motivations and agendas that you prefer to hide. Push past your mixed feelings so that they do not hamper your progress.

Emotional Shifts

As you flex your intuitive muscles, you'll eventually start to feel more secure and enjoy an enhanced sensitivity to life and to those around you. You'll begin to feel more alive, more aware of your physical surroundings. In moments when you feel carefree, habitual fears and negativity will fall away, and you may experience excitement for no apparent reason. At these times, business ideas will seem to flow easily, and problems will appear manageable. In fact, you may view problems that others have difficulty solving as a welcome challenge, allowing you to excel by using your intuitive skills to creatively handle difficult situations and people. As your intuitive capabilities blossom, you will find that these periods last longer. You'll learn to value being around enthusiastic or positive people who you now sense are supportive of you.

On the other hand, you may experience moments of some discomfort. You may find it more difficult—and even intolerable—to be around negative or dishonest people. For no apparent reason, you may experience moments of anxiety. These can be controlled and eliminated, as you will learn in Chapter 6, by learning to pinpoint the source. These periods will quickly pass. Hang on for the ride.

Thoughts That Are Not From You

You may come to realize that there are times when your thoughts may actually represent what someone else is thinking. Here's how it might happen. Assume you've been asked to develop a project idea to increase sales. After working on it, you're convinced of its viability. During a presentation to your business associates, however, you experience doubts. If you were comfortable about the idea before the presentation, you may be intuitively sensing a listener's concerns. Not realizing that this is a possibility, and unknowingly intuiting your listener's concerns, may cause your presentation to suddenly lack the confidence and enthusiasm needed to get your ideas across.

Negative People

If you accept the idea that you can intuit the thoughts of other people, it becomes easy to understand why living or working with negative people can disrupt your thinking and your equilibrium. Similarly, positive, supportive, or calm people evoke comforting feelings. If you've ever known someone whose presence you enjoy, you've experienced the effect of healing or positive thoughts. Negative people are toxic. Unconsciously intuiting their negative mindset can adversely affect your business performance.

If you don't realize that it's possible that you're picking up the negative thoughts of others, you may unconsciously block your intuitive channel to avoid these thoughts that are throwing you off. This blocking consumes energy that could be better put to more creative uses in your business life. If some business meetings exhaust you, consider that your sensitivity to others is causing you, without your realizing it, to unknowingly block thoughts that would hurt your feelings or disrupt you. If you have serious inner doubts about your business abilities, these thoughts can compound your worries and throw you into a tailspin. If, on the other hand, you feel confident, it's less likely that you'll be adversely influenced by another person's negative thoughts and, therefore, have to expend energy blocking them.

—A Technique—

Protecting Against Other People's Negative Thoughts

The next time you're with someone and start to feel uncomfortable, and find yourself having negative or discouraging thoughts for no apparent reason:

- Pay particular attention to how the person looks and acts. Does he or she have a frown or look tense?
- Ask some general questions to see if you can determine if the person is defensive or negative. For example, say to him or her, "Boy, it's a great day!" If the person is not in a good frame of mind, it's unlikely that he or she will respond in an enthusiastic manner.
- Take a moment and imagine that you can hear the person's thoughts. For example, say to yourself, "Here's what [*name of person*] is thinking," and let your imagined thoughts about what he or she is thinking flow through your mind. Are these thoughts destructive or negative in any way?

If you feel that this person is the source of your negative thoughts, try leaving the room and see how you feel. If leaving the room is not possible, converse about something light or humorous to see if this makes a difference. Cheering up or distracting a negative person can raise that person out of his or her rut—at least for a moment. If you feel better after the person has cheered up, there is a good chance that you were intuitively sensing his or her negativity, and that this was adversely affecting you. This insight can protect you from being unduly influenced by this person's negativity.

Upset People

Have you ever walked into a room full of people and, for no apparent reason, felt anxious or emotionally upset? If so, it's possible that you have picked up, and internalized, someone else's emotional state. Consciously empathizing with friends can have the same effect—you "catch" their emotional upset. So the next time your mood goes from good to bad when you walk into a room, consider the possibility that you have picked up another's distress. Not being aware of this possibility and experiencing bad feelings for no apparent reason can be confusing, even devastating. It is important to know when this is happening so that you can avoid being drawn into another's bad mood. Inheriting other people's negative emotions will block your intuitive instincts and limit your effectiveness in dealing with both them and the business process.

Adults can learn a great deal from children. Have you ever noticed how a child often senses another person's inner anxiety the moment he or she walks into a room. When this happen, adults are prone to tell children that their upset is imagined. In effect, the child is told to function in the world with less than his or her full sensing capabilities. Over time, the child naturally begins to doubt what he or she intuits and will often begin to repress these feelings. When these feelings cannot be repressed, there are often moments of confusion and a further shutting down of the child's sensing capabilities.

A number of years ago, a close associate of mine—I'll call her Pat—had a particularly difficult time coming to terms with her sensitivity to the feelings of other people. In an effort to become more of a hands-on manager, she started meeting with four of her senior managers every Monday morning. Although she felt fine before she walked into these meetings, she became anxious during the meetings for no apparent reason. Upon leaving the meetings, she felt fine.

She mentioned this casually to a management psychologist friend, Dr. Bench, over dinner one evening. He volunteered to attend the Monday morning meetings to see if he could pinpoint the cause of her anxiety. His initial guess was that some aspects of the business discussions were unconsciously making her uncomfortable. For ten weeks he tracked Pat's reactions at the meetings.

The pattern of anxiety continued. Pat was relaxed before each meeting, became anxious during all but two meetings, and was fine the moment she walked out. Dr. Bench detected that when Pat was talking to one manager—I'll call him Ted—she didn't look at him directly, something Pat was unaware of. As soon as Bench shared this, Pat realized that she was uncomfortable around Ted during the meetings. Bench checked the meeting minutes and discovered that Ted had missed the two meetings in which Pat was relaxed.

Pat invited Ted to lunch and, at the first opportunity, asked if he was having any problems that she could help him with. Ted nervously inquired if anyone had said anything to her about him. He then reluctantly admitted that he had a drinking problem that had worsened over the past six months. He was binge drinking on the weekends, and he was worried that someone would detect it at the Monday morning meetings. Pat assured him that he wouldn't be fired if he sought medical help. He seemed relieved. Pat's Monday morning meeting anxieties were alleviated.

Physical Experiences

Working with your intuition puts you more in touch with your body and its sensations. You may be aware of your feet touching the ground as you walk, and even, at times, sense the beating of your heart. And, over time, you will also notice that you experience distinct physical sensations when intuitive information is trying to break into your consciousness. If you're resisting your intuitive messages, another set of distinct sensations may occur, such as jumpiness around negative, evasive, and even untrustworthy people. There may even be tingling in your hands, sudden exhaustion, tightness in your neck or face, or other unusual or uncomfortable body feelings. These may result from inner stress created by your efforts to block your intuitive awareness. When that occurs, allow your thoughts free flow to see if you can identify any intuitive information you might be resisting.

—A Developmental Task—
Physical Patterns

Pay attention to any physical sensations that accompany apparently intuitive impressions. Keep track of them on a note pad.

Look for emerging patterns. Does your face flush when you are around positive people? What about any other physical feelings?

Physical sensations or reactions can help you connect with the threshold at which your hidden or oblique intuitive thoughts lie. You can then bring them clearly to the surface. These patterns may be individual to you and unlike those of other people exploring their intuitive abilities.

Discussing Your Efforts—Don't

You may feel the urge to discuss your progress with other people, but don't do so unless they themselves are accomplished in using their intuition. This means avoiding anyone who is still struggling to develop his or her intuition, those with doubts or concerns about its potential, those who are not completely comfortable with it, people who use it in a way that is destructive to other people, and those who believe that these abilities have some mysterious genesis. If in doubt, avoid a discussion.

The reasons for this rule are simple. Your particular intuitive experiences may be quite different from those other people have experienced, or know about. Engaging in a conversation may lead to confusion that can create stress. The more stress you're under, the more difficult it is to make progress. And the act of talking about what you're doing, what you hope to achieve, or what you have already achieved can drain critical energy away from your developmental efforts. In addition, people with undeveloped intuitive abilities may cause you to doubt your potential or what you're experiencing. They may discourage you by reinforcing old limitations that you're struggling to overcome. Those jealous of your emerging abilities could purposely say something to sabotage you. Or those frightened by what you may know about them may be openly critical of what you're doing.

Seven Stages—A Progress Road Map

Although developing your intuition is a personally distinct process, there are seven awareness stages that many people go through as their intuitive skills unfold. They are described below for you to use as a general progress benchmark. However, not being aware of experiencing any phase does not necessarily mean that you're not progressing. You may have unknowingly skipped a phase and not realize that you've jumped forward, or particular life stresses may have momentarily blinded you. Or the awareness phases simply may not be part of your developmental process.

To the extent that you become aware of these phases, you will notice that positive changes occur in your thinking, perception, motivation, feeling, and business and personal life goals. A word of caution: Each time you reach a new level, your awareness may be so enlightening that you may want to stop and wallow around where you are. Keep going, even if you're convinced that you have achieved all that's possible—or all that you need. Be alert for what will be inevitable stirrings inside you to push you forward. You'll find them at each awareness level. Don't ignore them. They're your signals that you're on the right path, and they're calling you forward. As you reach the more advanced awareness levels, interestingly enough, you'll be less inclined to stop along the way.

Here are the seven awareness, or insight, stages:

Insight Level One. This is the basic life awareness level for most people. At Level One, people are motivated, and ruled, by a set of beliefs about themselves and the world around them that has been passed on by parents, teachers, peers, and mentors. These beliefs are never questioned, unless, possibly, someone a person respects, such as an authority figure, an idol, or a human behavior expert, shows him or her otherwise, or the severity of the problems created by adhering to one or more of these beliefs forces the person to change his or her belief structure in order to survive. For people at Level One, life is a never-ending pursuit of goals that generations before them have established and approved as worthy. Depending on cultural beliefs, these goals may be money, personal power, recognition, or acceptance by other people. Virtually everyone at this level has enough awareness to survive economically and overcome life's obstacles despite his or her flawed belief system. When success comes, it is the result of sheer will power and hard work.

Insight Level Two. At Level Two, you begin to sense that everyday pursuits and goals won't be enough to bring lasting satisfaction. Typically, you will enter Level Two when you have struggled, and possibly achieved, enough to get an inkling that even if all your career, material, and relationship desires were fulfilled, something would still be missing. That feeling often results in an intense intellectual curiosity about new ideas and other ways to self-actualize. Using your intuition for business is one of these new possibilities. This is an exciting time. It's filled with purpose—that of uncovering the mind's potential, whatever that may be.

Insight Level Three. At this stage, you have acquired enough insight about how things are and how they work to feel pretty confident that there is more to your humanness than is traditionally thought of in your culture—that, for example, there is some form of mind skill that can be evoked to, say, control your destiny or achieve your goals in business. And that there is more to achieving than just working hard. You may, at this stage, feel that you have discovered the inside track on life in business—the hidden answers. Some people become somewhat egotistical about their new insights at Level Three, and feel a strong need not only to share their insights, but to bring other people up to their awareness level. Don't give in to this need. If you do, expending energy on trying to convince other people of your insights will slow you down. Keep the following thought in mind if you find yourself struggling at Level Three: The need to convert others comes from an inner need to accept new ideas within yourself.

Insight Level Four. Expect to struggle with yourself when you reach Level Four. At this consciousness plateau, you've subconsciously cleared many blocks, including false beliefs, that may have held your progress back. Your gut will tell you that you're definitely on to something. You can see the glimmer of light at the end of a still-long tunnel—that your new intuitive skill is more than an intellectual possibility. Although your gut tells you that you're on the right track, a part of you is still not ready to allow your innate potential to surface. There is inner resistance. This resistance often surfaces as an intellectual effort to understand your potential in the context of past learning. You may, for example, feel inclined to label any expression of your intuitive ability as an amazing coincidence. As you experience these coincidences more often, there will be a point when it will occur to you that they may not be what you thought: mere coincidences. That realization will be exciting, and will propel you forward even more adventurously. Be prepared to make some mistakes at this stage—particularly errors in judgment. But don't let the mistakes force you to retreat. These mistakes are a necessary part of your development. Don't doubt the direction you've taken. Be patient. Wait for the clouds to clear and the doubts to lessen. They will.

Insight Level Five. As the clouds clear from your mind in Level Four, encouraging feelings will follow. You will arrive at Level Five. There will be a wondrous sense of anticipation—like waiting for a prize drawing in a million-dollar giveaway contest. You'll be less negative about life. You'll feel that your inner potential is on the verge of blossoming. Solutions to problems you've wrestled with for years will pop into your mind. The obvious will reveal itself. And you will wonder what you must have been thinking about all those years. That difficult boss will become easy to handle. The confusion over career choices will vanish. You'll finally understand that you have had a hand in allowing these positive aspects to surface in your life. At this stage, you're solidly headed toward unleashing your full intuitive potential. But be careful. At Level Five, your new intuitive skill is not yet so firmly planted that the negative thoughts of others can't cause you to fall back—to lose your confidence. No matter what happens, persist in moving forward. Trust that you will continue to make progress. And, as in earlier stages, do not discuss what is happening, or your new insights, with anyone, unless you're absolutely sure that that person is clearly more advanced, is mentally and emotionally balanced, and is someone who will not be intimidated or threatened by or jealous of you.

Insight Level Six. You finally have made a significant intuition skill breakthrough. And you know it. This is a time to rest—the emotional effort required to clear away the blocks to your inner capabilities has been substantial. Level Six is the time to sit back and absorb what you've achieved. You'll notice a strong sense of security about your life in business, and in general. You'll notice that you no longer have any need to convince other people of your insights and realizations, or of your abilities. You can bask in what you have finally accepted. It was a long, hard struggle. Yet now, from your vantage point, you'll find it hard to believe that it was so difficult. You'll see how a simple change of awareness freed all blocks to intuition. You're now ready to move to the highest level.

Insight Level Seven. Refreshed from your Level Six rest, you're now ready to integrate the full use of your intuition, and the knowledge that comes with its use, in a way that makes your life in business, and in general, flow easily and effortlessly. You understand, and see in operation, how your thoughts and the thoughts of other people create the world you live in. With your new intuitive awareness, you'll be able to move yourself into work areas that best suit you, and in which you'll find the most fulfillment. In every way you'll move toward an environment that fits your temperament—one that just feels right in your gut. Any old emptiness will be gone, and you will finally know that you're connected with where you need to go and what you need to do. And you'll have access to the information that you need to get there—your intuition.

Conclusion

As your full intuitive potential becomes readily available to you, you may find that you experience a series of new physical and mental awarenesses. Don't let any new awareness or insight throw you off or slow you down. Any changes that occur are part of the natural process of releasing old limiting beliefs that have blocked your ability to use your intuitive gift effectively. Use them as benchmarks for your progress.

Chapter 4

How Your Intuition Talks to You: Gut Feelings, Flashes, and Other Intuitive Messages

"People usually know the right choices to make in business, but often, unknowing, let faulty logic or fear override their gut feelings."

—Patrick M.,
director of systems development

Recognizing True Intuitive Messages

Have you ever placed a bet on a horse that you felt was a sure winner and been wrong? Or approached a new business prospect with a gut feeling that you would walk away with a deal, but didn't? What about similar experiences that didn't work out in accordance with what you've felt or thought? In these cases, you've mistakenly relied on thoughts or feelings that did not come through your intuition, but rather originated elsewhere.

An important aspect of building your intuitive skills is learning to distinguish true intuitive information from thoughts or messages that appear to be intuitive, but actually originate from negative or other nonproductive thoughts, fears, anxieties, illusions, or past recollections. It's not unusual for people who have just lost their job to have a good feeling about the first new opportunity that comes along, a feeling that they attribute to their intuition, but that is often really due to relief. Unknowingly acting on faulty intuitive-appearing information not only increases your chances of a poor outcome, but if the outcome is poor, inhibits your willingness to trust your intuition.

In this chapter, you learn the typical and reliable ways in which your intuition conveys its information to you. In later chapters, we explore how to recognize what appear to be intuitive impressions and feelings, but have their source elsewhere. Mastering how to identify the differences between the two will give you the ability to quickly recognize true intuitive messages.

How Intuitive Information Surfaces

There are many in which ways your intuitive knowing or messages may surface into your conscious awareness. Paying attention to how your intuition talks to you will not only increase your awareness of your innate intuitive ability, but facilitate and expand your ability to work with it. You may find that you favor one form over the others. If so, cultivate it.

Let's explore the typical ways in which intuitive messages may surface. Keep in mind, however, that it's not always possible to precisely identify what particular type of intuitive knowing is in process. At times, it may be hard to distinguish between a gut feeling and a hunch. But that doesn't matter. The only thing that is important is recognizing that your intuition is trying to tell you something.

Gut Feelings

Most of us have encountered business situations that looked promising on the surface, but felt wrong in our gut. We have met people who appeared to be fair, but our gut told us were not. How your stomach reacts to ideas and situations is as important as how your thinking mind reacts to them. Gut feelings can be signals that you must further explore the situation and your intuitive reaction to it. Gut feelings can also be confirmations that a course of action or belief is intuitively correct or incorrect. The strong physical sensation of a gut feeling easily distinguishes it from other types of intuitive signals, such as thought flashes.

Gut feelings can tell you something immediate, or be a clue to something to come in the future. You might experience an uncomfortable twinge in your stomach just as you're about to sign a long-term business contract. You should heed this feeling and, before you sign, carefully rethink all aspects of the deal for potential problems. If you find yourself in this situation, excuse yourself. Find a quiet area, relax for a moment, and see if there are any unsettling or random thoughts in your mind that you have been ignoring or discounting in the rush to put the contract together. If so, allow them to surface fully. It's possible that in trying to get the deal done, you have blocked any intuitive messages to avoid uncovering issues that might create delays and added work. Or you may have ignored a gut feeling that the suppliers you're relying on to support your long-term contract commitment are about to raise their prices, and so entering into a long-term contract now may not be the best decision.

You can also use your gut sensitivity to intuitively assess what you want to know. Peter J., a food company executive, describes how this works:

> "I feel my intuition as a physical feeling in my gut. It's not something that kicks in at any time—rather, it happens only when I focus in on an issue that needs solving. Almost unconsciously I seem to be running various solutions past my gut, and it responds with one of two subtly different sensations, one sensation that means 'yes' and another that means 'no.'"

Gut feelings have a scientific basis. Some time ago Candace Pert, the chief of brain biology at the National Institute of Mental Health, came up with a theory that a brain neuromodulator called cholecystokinin, or CCK, a hormone involved in the digestive process as well as the learning and memory processes, may actually cause what we know as gut feelings. CCK is released after we've had a satisfying meal and sends that message to the brain for future memory use. It's thought by some researchers that when we mentally pick up intuitive clues, CCK is released in our digestive system, producing a gut sensation.

Intuitive Flashes

Nothing is more exciting than having an answer to a difficult business problem suddenly, and without effort, flash into your mind. Intuitive flashes, either visual images or thoughts, have produced many ingenious product and business ideas as far back as people can recall. Sir Isaac Newton, who discovered the laws of gravity, is well known to have first experienced his theories in intuitive flashes and then scientifically verified them through experimentation.

These flashes often appear as visual images, sudden mental "snapshots" of an event, situation, person, or idea. For example, while you are relaxing in a chair, the image of a new business product may suddenly pop into your mind. If that happens, pursue its viability. Whether they take the form of visual images or thoughts, intuitive flashes often convey all the information that we need—the total idea—in a complete mental package.

For many people, such as Jean F., a business consultant, their best ideas come in flashes when they least expect it:

> "I experience intuition as flashes, ideas—'ahas.' They usually occur when I least expect them to. There are times when I'm working on a problem, getting absolutely nowhere, and decide to drop everything and take a walk in the park. Almost magically, as soon as I start looking at the sky or watching birds, solutions flash into my mind."

Jean F. relies on intuitive insight flashes for business progress and success. When they occur for you, carefully consider them, or you may miss an opportunity.

Hunches

Hunches are nonphysical feelings you experience that tell you that something is about to happen, that you're missing an opportunity, or that a particular choice is right or wrong. You may have a hunch that a particular job is the right one for you, or that making a particular business decision would be wrong. Hunches can be predictive and are not accompanied by a strong physical component, as are gut feelings. Typically, you need to do some work to define what you're sensing, to consciously analyze your options. A hunch is generally not as information-specific as, for example, an intuitive flash, which typically delivers a "package" thought or image to the conscious mind. Interestingly, hunches may have an immediacy about them, making you feel that they must be acted upon now.

Georgia T., a business writer, often relies on her hunches about what book publishers may be interested in. She related the following incident that illustrates the importance of acting on hunches:

"For months I had been mulling over what might be a good subject for my next book. I had a hunch that one on business networking would be interesting, and I thought about asking a networking executive acquaintance, John G., if he would be willing to let me use articles I wrote for his networking newsletter. I decided to first speak to a book acquisition editor, who, although encouraging, felt that it might be a tough book project to sell because a lot of networking books were already on the market. His comments threw me off, so I delayed approaching John about the book idea. About a month later, John called me out of the blue, said that a major publisher had approached him to do a networking book, and asked if I would ghostwrite it for him for a flat fee. By not acting on my hunch, not only did I lose the source of ready material, but I also lost the chance to earn what could have been substantial royalties."

Dreams

Dreams, although often precognitive or synchronistic in nature, can also be the source of intuitive solutions to problems or questions you're confronting. A precognitive dream predicts a future event. A synchronistic dream occurs virtually simultaneously with the event. For example, you may be dreaming about someone whom you haven't seen in years when you're awakened by a telephone call from that very person. Very often, you must stretch to interpret what your dreams are telling you, but at times they can be very direct. Intuitive dreams provide you with insights, sometimes symbolically and sometimes allowing you to actually see, for instance, the solution to a business problem played out visually.

A great deal of research into the intuitive nature of dreams has been conducted, including a decade of research at the Maimonides Medical Center in New York by Dr. Stanley Krippner, now a psychology professor at Saybrook Institute in California, and years of research at the Duke University Parapsychology Laboratory by dream expert L. E. Rhine. This research has uncovered many cases verifying that dreams can contain precognitive and synchronistic aspects. If you're interested in learning about dreams and how to interpret their symbols, I recommend reading *Dreamworking*, written by Dr. Stanley Krippner and Dr. Joseph Dillard, and published by Bearly Limited.

Your Inner Voice

Intuitive messages delivered by what is often referred to as your inner voice are intuitive thoughts that appear as though someone else is talking to you, as opposed, for example, to intuitive flashes, which randomly surface sometime after you've posed a question for your intuition to work on. Finding your inner voice is nothing more than learning to control the timing of your intuitive answers.

There are a number of ways to get in touch with your inner voice. Here's a two-stage technique that you might try to see how it works for you.

—A Technique—

Finding Your Inner Voice

It is possible that you may be someone who experiences intuition as an inner voice. The next time you have to solve a business problem, try this exercise and see what happens. Do it in a quiet place, away from the telephone. Make sure there can be no interruptions. It's best if your clothing is loose and comfortable. Before you start, use the relaxation exercise below (or any other that works for you) to get your conscious mind into neutral, and to remove any mental noise. It might be useful to record these instructions on an audio cassette, with appropriate time intervals between steps, to avoid having to look at the book to see what to do next. Plan to spend about ten minutes doing the exercise.

The analogies used in this exercise are purposely nontraditional to help you begin to break patterns of thinking that may be blocking your intuitive process. Don't judge what you're being asked to do, see if you can let go and participate.

Stage I: Relaxation Technique (Five Minutes)

Sit in a comfortable chair and close your eyes. You're going to be taking five slow, deep breaths. Begin by inhaling slowly through your nose as you count to five, hold for a count of ten, and then slowly exhale for a count of five. Repeat this four times. If you don't find yourself starting to relax, repeat the entire process. When you have finished, sit quietly and feel your body slowly sinking into the chair. Concentrate on feeling your muscles relax. See if you can sense the muscles loosening until they are limp. Give yourself the time it takes to feel relaxed. It generally takes about two minutes, but don't put yourself on a time limit. That will create stress. Now count slowly back from ten. Each time you count a number, sense your body sinking farther into your chair. When you feel relaxed, imagine a warm breeze gently blowing across your body as you are sitting in the chair. Stay with this thought for at least one minute. (Do not worry about checking the time; the point is merely to slow down.) Enjoy each step and feel yourself dropping into a relaxed state.

Now picture yourself sitting on a sunny, sandy beach. There are no people or aspects of civilization in sight. You are facing the ocean. The waves are slowly rolling in. Behind you is a lush tropical forest. Imagine that you can hear the sound of the waves breaking on the shore. Smell the fresh sea air. Smell the soft, fragrant scent of tropical flowers. The sky above you is a warm, pale blue. If you have any worry or concern, make up a one-word name for it and place it in the middle of a pale blue bubble in your mind. Then imagine the bubble slowly and quietly floating out of the top of your head. Mentally, watch it float out. Do this for each worry or concern until you have let them all go. At this moment, you have no worries or concerns. Relax and enjoy the feeling of the ocean breeze as it gently moves over you. Relax.

Stage II: Accessing Your Inner Voice (Five Minutes)

When you are completely relaxed, imagine that you are floating upward. See yourself moving toward the heavens. Watch the earth slowly fade in the distance. The place where you are going is safe and free of all outside influences. Do not rush your trip. As you float upward, imagine that you're beginning to move toward a vast desert area. You can see a beautiful, majestic mountain off in the distance, in the middle of the desert area. When you're directly over the desert area, let yourself gently, and slowly, float downward, landing about one-quarter of a mile from the mountain. As you land on the desert, sit comfortably on the sand with your legs crossed, facing the mountain. Sense the power of the mountain. It contains tremendous energy. Nothing can damage it. As you are sitting there, imagine a wise old man in a long white robe floating down from above. Watch as he slowly descends. He lands about eight feet away from you and sits in the same position as you. Look at his appearance. His gentle face has a soft, warm expression. His eyes are a soft blue. He is clean-shaven, and he has long, white hair flowing softly over his shoulders. Greet him. Wait as he greets you back. Now ask him to assist you in solving whatever problem is confronting you, or in answering any question you have on your mind. Talk to him. Wait for his answers. Just listen for the thoughts that come as you sit there. When you think you have all the answers you need, or will receive, thank him for his help. Go over the answers carefully in your mind. Then imagine yourself slowly floating upward and back to the beach. When you arrive on the beach, sit there and go over the information again in your mind. When you have done this, imagine the sun slowly going down and begin to be aware of your chair.

Feel all the points of contact between your body and the chair. Open your eyes when you are ready. Take your time. Don't rush yourself. (If you do, you may get a slight headache.) Immediately write down all the thoughts that passed through your mind while you were sitting across from the old man. The old man is your inner voice talking to you. And the thoughts are your intuitive answers.

Finding Your Intuitive Style

As already suggested, intuitive messages can break into your conscious awareness in a number of ways—in the form, for example, of a physical feeling or a sense of knowing. If you're like most people, you'll find, particularly in the early stages of your intuitive development, that you have a natural inclination for one particular way. But you may not be like most people, and you may experience message breakthroughs in more than one way. So, be alert to your possibilities. Knowing your style will help you become more aware of when your intuition is working for you.

If you are a visually inclined person, you will experience intuitive messages predominantly in the form of mental images, such as in dreams or through mental pictures when awake. If your inclination is auditory, you will experience messages in the form of thoughts, sometimes referred to as your inner voice. A knowing-inclined person simply knows, or senses, the information. And a feeling-inclined person connects with his or her intuitive information through physical sensations, such as a gut feeling. Interestingly, how you generally approach communicating with other people is a clue to your intuitive inclination. For example, if you have a visual inclination, you talk in terms of seeing. You make statements like, "Let me *see* if I can figure the problem out." If you're inclined toward sensing through feelings, you might say something like, "I wish I could *put my finger on* the solution." If you're an auditory person, you might use statements like, "I *hear* you." If you have a knowing inclination, you might make statements like, "It just *seems* to be the right thing to do."

In addition, the form of your intuitive messages may change depending on the particular circumstances, your developmental progress, or your emotional state. For example, your intuitive messages may almost always surface as a gut sensation. However, as you work with your intuition, you may experience messages in the form of thoughts, such as someone's name popping into your mind for no reason at all. And, eventually, messages may come through predominantly as visual flashes. Whatever your inclination—and everyone starts with at least one natural preference—don't attempt to steer yourself toward any approach. Relax and let it happen.

—An Exercise—

What's Your Intuitive Style?

Do you have an intuitive sense preference? Well, let's explore this possibility. Most people lean strongly toward one preference— visual, knowing, auditory, or feeling. You may find that you experience your intuitive messages in more than one way, or that your preference changes depending on the circumstances. Plan on spending five minutes with the following exercise. It will help you identify your intuitive style.

Single out someone you know with whom you currently have a good relationship. It could be someone you haven't seen for years, or a business associate. Do not choose a loved one, such as a spouse or child. And do not pick someone occupying the building or home where you're doing this exercise.

With this person in mind, sit in a comfortable chair, close your eyes, and relax, using, if necessary, the relaxation exercise on page 56.

When you are relaxed, with your eyes still closed, think about the person you've identified. Get the person fixed in your mind. Ask the person a question about something you'd like to know about him or her, and wait for a response. Let your thoughts about the person flow freely for two to three minutes to see what comes into your mind.

When you feel like stopping, open your eyes and make a written note of everything that occurred. As you began to fix the person in your mind, did you have a clear mental picture of him or her? Did you experience any physical sensations, such as a sensation in your chest, a sense of warmth around you, or a tightening of your muscles? What about any thoughts that entered your mind in answer to your questions?

If you're a visual person, you experienced a clear mental picture of this person. If you have an auditory inclination, you may have experienced a thought message, as though he or she were talking to you. If you have a kinesthetic (feeling) inclination, you had a distinct physical feeling. If you have a knowing inclination, you simply know the answer to the question you asked.

Conclusion

Your intuition can communicate with you in one or more of a variety of ways: through a physical feeling, an auditory or visual message, or a sense of knowing—or a way that is unique to you. If you can identify your particular intuitive style, it will increase your awareness of when your intuition is sending a message.

Part Two

Six Steps to Developing Your Intuition for Business

Chapter 5

Step 1:
Clear Thought Static

"Preoccupation with my problems often blocks seeing obvious solutions."

—Jack R.,
marketing executive

Have you ever been so preoccupied with a problem or other issue that you've walked past people you know without seeing them? Or been introduced to someone and not heard the person's name when it was told to you? Undoubtedly, this has happened to you from time to time.

When you're lost in your own thoughts, particularly negative, obsessive, or other nonproductive ones, you limit your perceptive abilities. It's like trying to listen to a radio crackling with heavy static. It's very difficult, if not impossible. So, for example, if you're facing a business problem and you're mulling over one solution after another, intuitive information cannot break through into your conscious awareness. Recall those times when you cannot remember where you left something. Only when you relax, and stop trying to figure out where you could have left it, does the answer come to you.

To release your intuitive potential, then, you must learn to identify and clear all thought static. This chapter will show you how to do that. It is the first of six steps to permit the full release of your full intuitive potential that you will learn to take in Part Two.

Awareness: The Key to Eliminating Thought Static

Your mind must be occupied with something, and studies have shown that for much of the time, it is filled with negative or nonproductive thoughts. These thoughts, which I'll call mental static, can distort or block your conscious awareness of your intuitive messages. You can clear these thoughts by realizing that you have a choice over what fills your mind. In fact, your natural inclination is to be free of any such destructive thoughts. A helpful analogy is to compare your mind to a room. A room can hold only a limited number of people. And your mind can hold only one conscious thought at a time. If it's crowded with thought static, your intuitive messages cannot gain access.

Unfortunately, for many people, keeping their minds clear of mental static is not always easy. Living or working in a destructive environment and external negative influences contaminate their thinking. Have you ever started the day in a terrific frame of mind, and arrived home feeling in the dumps because you've been exposed to a negative or difficult co-worker or boss? If so, you've experienced firsthand what a destructive environment can do. By keeping nonproductive thoughts from encroaching on your mind space, however, you permit positive thoughts to automatically fill your conscious mind. These support the flow of intuitive information. Notice that when you're feeling positive and confident about your job, it's easier to generate creative business ideas or to solve problems.

The Mind-Clearing Challenge

The problem facing many people is that their minds have been filled with mental static for so long that they have become desensitized to it. It's like moving next to a busy airport or highway. At first, the noise drives you crazy, then you adjust to it and learn to tune it out. In so doing, you shut down a part of your conscious mind's sensing mechanism. By learning to pay attention to the noise in your mind, however, you will have the ability to take control and quiet it.

—A Technique—

Becoming Aware of Your Mental Static

The first step in clearing your mind of thought static is to sensitize yourself to the amount of mental static you generate daily. Here's a technique to help you.

Set aside five minutes every day for the next five days and pay attention to the negative and other nonproductive thoughts going through your mind. Write them down on a note pad. This will help you pull them fully into your conscious awareness. Pick a different time each day to do this. The first day, do it when you rise in the morning. The next day, do it right after lunch. Choose the periods randomly. Let your intuition steer you. The more aware you become of the flood of nonproductive thoughts racing through your mind, the more amazed you will be that you can pay attention to *anything* else at all.

A Technique for Cleaning Your Mind's Room

Once you start to realize, or sensitize yourself to, how much mental static you've allowed yourself to entertain, the next step in clearing your mind of these thoughts is to realize that they serve no useful purpose for you—and, in fact, hold you back in business by limiting your ability to be creative and to access your intuition. Only then can you take the next step necessary to clear your mind so that intuitive messages can surface.

Here's a technique for clearing your mind.

—A Technique—

Cleaning Your Mind's Room

When you become fully aware of how useless it is to allow unproductive thoughts to parade through your mind, you will naturally start to eliminate them. Set aside fifteen minutes a day for the next five days to work with the following mind-cleaning technique. This should be performed in a place where you won't be disturbed.

Sit in a comfortable chair. Close your eyes. Pay attention to each and every thought going through your mind. Spend about one minute doing this. Then see if you can stop all your thoughts, empty your mind completely, have it blank—and keep it totally blank for one minute. Were you successful? Undoubtedly, you found it impossible.

Now close your eyes again and spend four minutes examining the type of thoughts you have. See how many negative or otherwise nonproductive thoughts you recognize. Do not read further until you have done this. Were you able to identify any thoughts about past failures? How about any negativity regarding your future goals, such as your goal of developing your intuitive skills? Anything else?

This done, with your eyes still closed, stop contemplating anything negative or otherwise nonproductive. Allow yourself to dwell only on positive and other productive thoughts.

If you have trouble blocking any nonproductive thoughts, forcefully say the word *cancel* as each occurs. This will help you block them. As you eliminate all nonproductive thoughts, you will notice that you will begin to physically relax. Spend five minutes doing this.

When you're done, spend five minutes letting your thoughts go again in any direction. Actively introduce negative thoughts. Notice that your body tension increases. You may feel your facial muscles tighten. Nothing outside you has to change. Interestingly, body tension and negative thoughts go hand in hand. The more negative you are, the more tense your body, and vice versa. By eliminating negative thoughts, you relax, and by relaxing, you eliminate negative thoughts. The fact is that as body and emotional tension increase, creativity and intuitive capabilities decrease.

As you experiment with this technique, you will learn to gain control over your mental static, so that you can clear it when you want to access your intuition.

Welcoming Negative Thoughts

In spite of the obvious detrimental effect, there are some people who welcome negative thoughts with open arms, even when these thoughts guarantee failure. The reason: They offer many emotional benefits. Thinking negatively can be a clever way to ensure failure so that you can ignore uncomfortable emotional issues. Lack of success can be a solid way of avoiding rejection by friends or family who are struggling, or uncomfortable feelings that we've done better than our parents.

Thinking negatively may be a way to eliminate the anxiety of anticipating outcomes. By being negative and deciding not to try, you take fewer risks and, thus, have fewer outcomes to worry about. This keeps you emotionally safe, preventing you from moving out of what you perceive to be the known into the unknown.

The stress of having to solve a business problem can be overwhelming, especially when you think your career or business is at stake. A problem can make you confront, consciously or unconsciously, your deepest and most irrational fears: that you are not smart, not able to find a solution, or not able to make a go of an entrepreneurial business. Consequently, it is often much less stressful to avoid trying to be successful by being negative. It is imperative that at some point, you combat any fear of failure; otherwise you will never get past it.

A negative or failure-oriented philosophy occasionally can make you look like a hero in your own eyes, and in the eyes of others. People who are able to foretell the future are in great demand. So, if your only objective is to be a hero in business, be a negative person. It's easy to predict bad results, particularly if you have a hand in them.

Being negative can also make you feel good. Over lunch with business associates, have you ever participated in a discussion in which everyone listed one reason after another why a particular project was doomed? If so, did you experience a sense of excitement or power? If not, how about any other gratifying feelings? If you've never tried this, I urge you to do so to see what it feels like. If you have difficulty getting into the swing of it, invite an experienced business naysayer.

And, finally, negative talk is a way to gain peer acceptance; however, it will eventually taint your positive thoughts. Do you remember the discussions about how everyone did that followed taking a school exam? Those who performed well were often reluctant to say so for fear of being socially excluded. It can be the same in a competitive business environment. Peer pressure can push us into a negative pattern, especially when we are around people who do not know how to achieve their business potential. You may have a tendency to tell others who are having a tough time that you are also, to ensure that they accept you as a peer. Over time, this can become a bad habit that is hard to break.

Negative thinking may surface as you develop your intuition. In effect, it can be a fast gun for hire that gives you an excuse not to follow the gut feelings that you can't support in a traditional manner. In a nutshell, negative thoughts about your intuitive possibilities can give you the ultimate business rationalization for not pursuing them. Make every effort to avoid indulging in negative thinking.

Being Negative Without Knowing It

Many people are negative and don't know it. Some individuals who are unconsciously negative typically seek advice from people who call themselves realists, and who invariably find a problem with everything. These covert negative types always make "If only I had done . . ." or "If she or he had only let me . . ." statements. This often plays out in family situations, where the unconsciously negative person tends to seek out opinions from an overtly negative parent, spouse, or loved one. In this way, he or she can always blame that person for deterring them rather than acknowledging his or her own underlying negativity.

—A Test—

Are You Negative?

If you answer "yes" to any of the following questions, you may have a negative tendency that can distort your intuitive abilities.

1. Are you uncomfortable about the possibility of being labeled a negative thinker?
2. If someone suggests that you're thinking negatively, do you go to great lengths to tell him or her why this isn't true?
3. When someone suggests that you're thinking negatively, do you experience a gripping or other physical sensation in your stomach?
4. Do you frequently turn for advice to someone who is generally negative about new ideas, or who always throws cold water on your ideas?
5. Do you go out of your way to justify a negative position, such as stating that you're only evaluating the pros and cons of the situations?
6. Do you feel very uncomfortable being around negative people?

The realization that you are negative may be hard to accept. But if you ignore the possibility, you'll miss the chance to eliminate negative tendencies. Only if you acknowledge them will they go away.

Here's a technique you can use to break negative thought patterns.

—A Technique—

Breaking Negative Thought Patterns

Breaking negative thinking habits is difficult, but possible.

Set aside ten minutes each day for the next five days to explore your negative thoughts in depth. Pick a time when you won't be disturbed. Write down on a piece of paper all your negative thoughts, whether about the past, present, or future.

Then close your eyes and concentrate on exploring each negative thought. Thoroughly mull each over in your mind, taking it to its worst extreme. For example, if you're concerned that you're about to lose a business opportunity, explore all the negative implications. Be creative and expansive. Take them to their worst—and most ridiculous—extreme. Even dream up outrageous negative outcomes.

Here's how it works. Your first concern might be embarrassment over losing the opportunity. Next, say that it's going to hurt your career. Next, say that you'll never recover from this loss, and that it will scar your business career forever. Finally, say that once the president of the United States learns about what has happened he or she will publicly embarrass you by pointing out your total ineptness on his or her Saturday morning radio show. Then proceed to the next negative thought, and exaggerate it with equal vigor.

If at the end of five days you do not begin to see how ridiculous negative thinking is, spend an additional five days doing this exercise. Eventually, it will dawn on you how fruitless negative thinking is. You will also find that the majority of what you're negative about is so ridiculous or petty that you cannot believe you've turned over a portion of your life to its pursuit. When this happens, (and chances are good that it will), it will help break any inclinations toward destructive or negative thinking. Positive thoughts will automatically flow into your mind. Your mind will be receptive to your intuitive guide.

Use this technique whenever you fall back into a negative thinking pattern.

The Destructive Side of Positive Thinking

It's inconceivable that the most acclaimed attitude elixir, *positive thinking*, could have any drawbacks. There is no doubt that if you approach something negatively, there is little chance that it will work out. So, it's easy to relate to the concept that thinking positively is a key to success. Why, then, do things often not work out even when you're sure that you have successfully maintained a positive attitude? The answer to the next question will provide a clue. Did thinking positively require a constant conscious effort on your part? It could be that you have been so obsessively cluttering your mind with positive thoughts that intuitive messages cannot get through.

To allow your intuition to surface, in effect, you have to

learn to allow your mind to go into neutral—to let go of any need to actively and continually generate positive thoughts. If you find yourself constantly working at staying positive during the business day, you may be interfering with your intuitive workings. What's the answer? You must learn to maintain a positive *frame of reference*, rather than frantically trying to think positively. Maintaining a generally positive frame of reference means simply knowing that, no matter what happens, it's for the best. In other words, when results seem to go contrary to your conscious desires, accept that they are the right results for your intended direction and growth, provided you haven't been self-destructive. For example, if you lose a major sale, that may be the incentive you need to reexamine and improve your basic marketing approach, something that perhaps you should have done long ago. Maintaining a generally positive frame of reference becomes effortless as you learn to trust your intuitive guide.

—A Technique—
Creating a Positive Frame of Reference

Here's how to create a positive frame of reference. Assume that even though you're generally positive, you find yourself consciously preparing for possible disappointment in a business situation.

1. Fully acknowledge your concern by making a written note of it on a piece of paper or a note pad.
2. Take a close look at what you're feeling and why. Don't be afraid that by doing so your fears will be confirmed.
3. Don't try to overcome your underlying fears by forcing yourself to think positively. Pushing yourself to think positively is, in effect, nothing more than putting a new coat of paint over a rusty car body, and it gives your negative tendencies even greater strength. It's like telling a perverse person not to do something. The more you insist, the greater the chance that he or she may defy you.

4. Adopt a *positive frame of reference* by saying to yourself that no matter what the outcome of the business situation, it is destined for your personal growth.
5. Welcome a result that you think you may not be happy with, because it will provide a course correction or rerouting opportunity for your business development. Write down the following statement next to your concern.

> "I welcome whatever result occurs.
> It will provide me with a unique
> opportunity for growth and progress."

Above all, remember that if you do not acknowledge your negative feelings, you will lose the battle with any destructive inclinations that block your intuitive channel.

Conclusion

The first step in clearing your mind of unproductive thoughts that prevent intuitive messages from surfacing into your consciousness is to be aware of how much you may permit these thoughts, particularly negative thoughts, to occupy your mind. Once you become aware of what is happening, it's important that you take action to break what in effect is a bad thinking habit and clear your mind of thoughts that have no value in your business life.

Chapter 6

Step 2: Control Destructive Emotions

"I don't rely on my intuition when I am emotionally upset, because I can't trust what I'm sensing. I try to back off until the dust is settled."

—Peter K.,
manufacturing executive

Emotions and Your Intuition

When you're taken over by upsetting emotions, you cannot function at your peak in business, or in life in general. You become preoccupied, sometimes obsessed, with what's bothering you. Your mind is no longer clear. Your decisions tend to gratify your emotional needs, rather than your best business interests. You're no longer rational. Have you ever tried to solve a business problem when you were very upset? It's difficult, and sometimes impossible. Making matters worse, anxiety and other emotional conflicts prevent the flow of intuitive information into your awareness, further crippling your problem-solving abilities.

When you're relaxed, and your mind is not filled with anxieties, fears, or other emotional clutter, your intuitive ideas can break through. That's why some of your best ideas surface when you're taking a leisurely Sunday walk in the country or in the park. By simply increasing your awareness of how and when you're succumbing to counterproductive emotional issues, you'll be able to make the necessary mental adjustments to clear your mind.

In this chapter, you'll learn how to identify and effectively handle emotional conflict—fears, anxieties, and other destructive emotions—that interfere with the full release of your intuitive potential. Emotional conflict not only prevents the flow of your intuitive messages into your conscious, but often is the source of feelings and thoughts that are misinterpreted as intuitive messages, leading you further astray. Those who were continually let down by parents or other adults in childhood often develop a deep mistrust in humanity. Sadly, in dealing with people, they may mistake the apprehension arising from their general lack of trust as their intuition steering them away from those around them.

—A Quick Test—

Is It Intuition or Your Emotions?

Were you ever due a pay raise and were sure you wouldn't get it when, in fact, you did? Or had a great business idea flash into your mind, but let a friend convince you that it wouldn't work, only to later read about someone else making millions with the same idea? In the first case, your feeling was not the result of your intuitive knowing. In the second case it was, but you were afraid to trust it.

Trusting your intuitive knowing means learning to separate emotionally based thoughts from intuitive messages. Here's a quick way to learn to do that.

When you experience what appears to be an intuitive message, determine whether you are:

1. Tense
2. Actively analyzing the situation for a solution
3. Working with a manipulative or negative person
4. Desperate for a solution
5. Experiencing fear or anxiety
6. In a hurry
7. Trying to impress someone
8. Feeling bad about yourself
9. Overtired

If the answer to any is, "Yes, I am," there is a good chance that your message is originating from a nonintuitive source—possibly emotionally based.

Emotions in Business

There is no doubt that the emotional makeup of an individual dictates his or her business success or failure. When you're unaware of the power any destructive emotions may have over you, your business success is at risk. Think about the situation where a key manager has an "off" day and expresses doubts about the future of the business. This can be very unsettling for subordinates. Some may be able to manage their anxiety, but others may be consumed by it, becoming discouraged. They may worry about whether their job is secure, or whether they'll have the money to buy the new car or house they've been planning on. In either case, their concerns are unfounded. The business hasn't collapsed. The marketplace hasn't changed. But when people are taken over by irrational and unproductive emotions, it's often hard for them to deduce this. If the manager's poor attitude persists, the subordinates' anxiety may actually affect the manager. Because of the manager's low energy state, he or she can be pulled down further. Once the cycle starts, it is hard to break. If the unproductive emotional environment persists, the business will eventually be affected.

Recognition

There are almost as many theories about the causes of emotional issues as there are therapists to treat them. And the theories continue to evolve from year to year. So, attempting to discuss *why* we work the way we do is of little value. Leave that to the psychologists and psychiatrists.

One reason many people often have difficulty recognizing what is necessary in order to remove inner emotional conflict is that they are taken over by the anger they feel toward the person or persons that created their problem. So they trap themselves, never letting go of the anger long enough to pay attention to doing what is necessary if they are to heal. How many times have you blamed your parents for dumping some emotional hang-up on you that you're convinced has held you back? By the same token, how many times have you been aware enough to see that your parents were in the same spot as you are? They had unfair emotional issues dumped on them before they knew what was happening. Should you then blame your grandparents? Where does it stop? A parent with an emotional hang-up is no different from a parent with a genetic problem: It will undoubtedly be passed on to his or her children. Sometimes the labels change, but the results are always the same: unhappiness in one form or another. What changes is our method of covering up underlying issues.

The key to removing destructive emotions that are inhibiting access to your intuitive potential is to recognize *how* you work emotionally and when you are overtaken by emotional conflict. This is not always easy. Usually, any emotional conflict you have has developed subtly over a lifetime. In addition, you may even have unknowingly embraced it in order to blot out life issues and awarenesses that cause emotional pain and anxiety.

It is easy to detect the presence of emotional conflict when business situations confuse you or make you self-conscious. The first two of the following three techniques will help you begin to identify possible emotional conflict. If you do uncover any, use the third technique to work around it. Understanding your emotional workings in any type of business situation lays the necessary foundation for seeing where emotional conflict may be present in other types of situations.

Technique 1

—A Technique—
Identifying Emotional Conflict

When you encounter a business situation or statement that confuses you—for example, one of your best managers is performing poorly for no apparent reason—your confusion may be a clue that underlying anxiety or other unsettling emotional issues, already discussed, are blocking your intuitive channel.

Try the following technique when you find yourself in a situation that is confounding you.

1. Go somewhere where you'll be undisturbed and relax, using the relaxation exercise on page 56, if necessary.
2. Consciously welcome your confusion as a clue that there may be an unsettling emotional issue within yourself that you are not acknowledging.
3. Consciously accept the possibility that you might prefer not to know why this is occurring.
4. Say out loud or write the following statement:
   "I know that I'm blocking something I need to know."
5. Now let your thoughts flow freely, no matter how nonsensical they seem. In fact, stretch to see how many outlandish thoughts come to mind. Write them down on a note pad. Don't try to limit your search to logical explanations. See if you can identify any emotional issues, fears, or anxieties that may be preventing you from eliminating the confusion.

In the case of a manager who is performing poorly, for example, you may find that you are reluctant to learn that he or she is fed up with the job and wants to quit. That would force you to work hard to find a replacement, a burden considering your current workload.

If you have identified any emotional conflict, use Technique 3 to free yourself of its influence.

Technique 2

Here's an exercise to help you begin the process of identifying your emotional conflict in a business setting without awaiting an actual situation.

—An Exercise—
Identifying Emotional Conflict

Imagine yourself in the following situation and see what feelings and resulting thoughts you experience.

Assume you are a senior executive for a large manufacturing company. Right after lunch today, you have an extremely important business meeting with a prospective customer. This will be your first meeting with him, and your job is to convince him that your company can handle a major project for him. At lunch, the waitress accidentally spills salad oil on the front of your shirt and tie. There is no time to change your shirt or tie.

Take a moment and jot down on a note pad what your thoughts and feelings are as you contemplate going to the business meeting with these very noticeable food stains on your clothes. Would you be self-conscious about your appearance? Would it affect your self-confidence? Remember, each time you're in a situation where you are worrying about what others may think, you're blocking your intuitive channel. This self-consciousness could make it appear as though you lack the confidence necessary to handle the project. And your emotional conflict could make you unable to intuit the best way to establish a solid rapport with your prospective customer.

If this situation were real and emotional conflict was present, you would use Technique 3 to free yourself of its influence.

Technique 3

Once you've identified emotional issues that potentially block your intuition, here's a technique to help break their influence.

—An Unlocking Technique—
Eliminating Nonproductive Emotions

Use the following technique to unblock any emotional barriers to your intuitive messages. Do not concern yourself with why or how the technique works. Just go with it without thinking about it.

Once you have identified emotional conflict in a business situation, get a piece of paper and draw a line down the center of it.

Record all your thoughts and feelings as you consider the situation. Put the positive thoughts and feelings in the right-hand column, and the negative thoughts and feelings in the left-hand column. You must be totally honest with yourself. No matter how ridiculous the thought or feeling, write it down. After you have finished, review the list carefully.

Now close your eyes and relax, using, if necessary, the relaxation technique on page 56. With your eyes still closed, imagine tearing the sheet of paper in half and throwing the portion with the negative thoughts and feelings into a raging fire. Visualize the paper being consumed by the fire.

The symbolic burning of all negative thoughts and feelings helps clear your conscious mind of emotional conflict. And, since your subconscious mind responds most effectively to symbolic messages, its tremendous power is also enlisted.

Reconsider the business situation, such as finding a solution to a marketing problem, in which you want assistance from your intuition. Let your thoughts flow freely again, no matter what they are. Do not block or resist any thoughts, even if they appear unrelated. When negative or other destructive thoughts or feelings surface, immediately and emphatically say, "Cancel." And stay relaxed, even if you experience a blank period. Answers that you have never considered will begin to come into your mind. When you've finished gathering your thoughts, write them on your note pad.

The more you try this technique, the quicker the results will come. Your goal is to quickly clear emotional blocks.

Fear and Anxiety—Major Intuition Roadblocks

Fear and anxiety are part of our world. We have discussed how they block and distort intuitive messages. When you are anxious or afraid, it's difficult to distinguish intuitive messages from thoughts generated by your fear or anxiety. When you are in a frightened state, you often expect the worst—a feeling usually founded in your imagination, not your intuition. Your mind often cannot distinguish between fear-induced and intuitive messages, because they surface in the same form as thoughts or images. So, be careful when you are in a frightened or anxious state, it's unlikely that the messages are intuitive.

A great deal of damaging anxiety often comes from what we perceive to be personal shortcomings. If this is true for you, accepting yourself, no matter what, and realizing that what you believe to be a failing is nothing more than a difference between you and someone else is the answer. If you don't do this, your most powerful business tool, intuition, is turned off. Accepting the way you are allows you to relax and clear your mind. For instance, if you are not *the* smartest person in the world, so what?

Letting Go of Fears and Anxieties

Initially, learning to easily let go of fears or anxieties is difficult, especially for those who always worry excessively about making the right choices. In a convoluted way, worry frequently seems to provide a sense of comfort. For some, the more they worry about a problem, the more effort they feel they're making to solve it.

If this is true for you and you're finding it hard to quiet these emotions, try to identify each worry or anxiety you're experiencing. For example, when confronted with a worrisome problem, see if you're afraid that you won't find a solution. Or, if somehow you feel that the act of worrying assures you that a solution is possible. Look for any other self-destructive feeling, such as a sense of being overwhelmed; chances are you'll see it's an irrational one. If it is, recognizing it as such will assist you in letting it go.

Here's how Patty D., the president of her own computer software firm, describes one of her primary business worries, and what she does when it surfaces:

> "I frequently worry irrationally about money. I start to think that being a salaried employee would be more financially secure. When this concern gets out of hand, I say to myself, 'Patty, how likely is it that every source of revenue is going to dry up?' That brings reality back, and I can immediately let go of my worry."

Not everyone can work through their irrational fears as easily as Patty. They must go to greater lengths to calm their minds. If this is you, here's a technique to help you let go of worries.

—A Technique—
Clearing Worries

The next time you're confronted with a business dilemma and cannot clear yourself of worrisome feelings, tell yourself that you are going to stop worrying for just one minute. Before you begin, make a firm commitment to go back to your worries as soon as the minute is over. Time yourself. Don't attempt to remain worry-free for more than one minute.

The next time you use this technique, set aside two worry-free minutes. And each additional time you try this approach, extend the time that you intend to remain worry-free by one more minute. Don't go beyond five minutes. If you find that you're having difficulty extending the period of time, go back to a time period you found manageable.

The point of this technique is not to see how long you can remain worry-free, but to realize that you can stop worrying when you so choose.

This technique works because you are not attempting to immediately force a major change in what may be a deeply ingrained emotional pattern. The part of you that may like to worry knows that all is not lost, and will not resist the momentary change. Ultimately, you'll be surprised at how easy it is to stop worrying on demand.

Irrational Worries

Irrational worries are particularly destructive to career and business progress and satisfaction. There are those who live comfortably, but are continually and irrationally worried about being broke. Their only relief comes from distracting themselves with frenetic pursuits, which might include chasing members of the opposite sex or other compulsive activities. When you are overtaken by out-of-balance emotional needs, you lessen or eliminate the conscious flow or recognition of intuitive messages. If this happens to you, the answer is to learn to see how unfounded your worries are.

Are you ready for a technique that can help?

—A Technique—

Letting Go of Irrational Worries

When you find yourself consumed by an overpowering worry, determining that it is irrational will help clear it. Here's how to do that.

Go where you won't be disturbed, and spend five minutes writing down all your feelings on a note pad. Be totally honest with yourself.

Assume that for days you've been so anxious about whether or not you would get a promotion that you've been hoping for that you haven't been able to think about, or do, anything productive. This morning your boss just told you that you would not be promoted. Now write down what you feel, such as, I feel:

1. Hopeless about my career
2. Depressed over my poor finances
3. Like a loser
4. I'll never have the things I want

By simply fully acknowledging all your feelings in writing, it becomes easier to analyze whether or not your worry is irrational—and, in a case like our hypothetical situation, in fact, all is not lost.

By eliminating irrational and unfounded worries or other preoccupations, you free yourself to address those that may have a real basis. And you give your intuitive guide an opportunity to send you some help. In our example, it may suddenly occur to you to return to school, a strategy you had not seriously considered before, or an idea to increase sales may surface and put you back in the running for promotion.

Difficulties in Uncovering Any Self-Destructive Tendencies

As you now know, some emotional needs can be so overpowering that they can dictate your business decisions without your realizing it. If they happen to be destructive, they can derail you and your intuition.

Problematic emotions, such as lack of confidence, commonly hold people back. To make matters worse, these people often repress the awareness of their low self-esteem by manufacturing unfounded reasons why they should remain in low-paying or unfulfilling business situations. Tackling their poor self-image creates more discomfort than the pain of having only a marginal career. And so they become stuck, choosing to stick with a pain that is familiar rather than to progress and overcome their emotional obstacles.

Marion T., a sales manager for a large automotive parts distributorship, developed a very creative way of getting in her own way:

> "My tendency to always look ahead blocks me. I'm very intuitive about business situations, and can often readily see future outcomes. Unfortunately, my tendency to want to keep looking ahead prevents me from paying attention to the day-to-day here and now. I envision the end result, and become impatient about making it happen. Instead of plugging away at achieving it, I find I would rather move on to the next vision or concept."

Marion's self-defeating habits create anxiety, which impedes her progress. She rationalizes that it's more interesting to move to the next idea than to complete what she intuits would be successful. It is likely that Marion unconsciously prefers to hide from the inner conflict that comes with seeing a project through, even though this habit robs her of ultimate success. Marion's problem is not uncommon. This type of self-sabotaging behavior can be avoided by fully acknowledging your feelings.

Clues to Hidden Emotional Conflict

The awareness that destructive emotional issues may be in play is generally all that is necessary to identify the issues and clear away your blocks. But very often these emotional issues are based upon beliefs that have been so ingrained that you don't question their truth or their basis. They are so buried in your subconscious that it's often impossible to readily identify them. In these cases, simply knowing that there may be an unidentified emotional issue creating emotional conflict can be sufficient to remove its control over you. The way to identify this hidden source of emotional conflict is to learn to recognize clues to its existence and end-run it.

For example, assume that you want to start your own business but are reluctant to do so because you have trouble dealing with people and you don't know why. The solution is not to waste time figuring out why you have this problem. Simply end-run it by considering a partnership with a person who is good with people. Getting started with someone like this provides you with a good role model. In addition, it will get you on your feet as an independent businessperson quickly. Once you're financially on your way, you then can spend the time necessary to resolve the issue for yourself.

Thinking, talking, and acting destructively are obvious clues that you are in the grip of underlying emotional issues that block your intuition. Some clues are less obvious. Here are some of these less-obvious clues.

Constant Complaining

Complaining can be an essential part of the business day for many. Lunchtimes are great opportunities to voice whatever you are unhappy with. Once someone starts the ball rolling, complaints start coming out of the woodwork. At times, doing this is relatively harmless, but when it's chronic, it may be a clue to a hidden emotional conflict.

Obviously, some complaints are legitimate. Complaints to management may address problems that need to be resolved so that morale and productivity stay high. However, there are other complaints that may have nothing to do with what is really troubling you, but are a smoke screen behind which lies your real upset. If you are unchallenged by your job, for example, and feel unable to correct this, your frustration may manifest itself through complaints about a series of unrelated issues, such as lack of support by your management or uncommitted co-workers.

The complaining that masks your frustration clogs your intuitive channel and litters your mind with unproductive thoughts. So, when you take your own complaints at face value, you run the risk of hampering your business progress. The key is to dig deeply to find the real issue behind your complaint.

Listening to and being sucked into another's complaints can be equally damaging. We've all encountered the type of chronically unhappy employee who gripes about everything. Such a person might approach you with, for instance, the complaint that the company doesn't seem to care about its employees. You list the many efforts taken to improve employee conditions. The person remains unconvinced. Feeling frustrated, you counter the complaints with more facts. This strategy seldom works with this kind of complainer, because although he or she does not know it, these complaints are a smoke screen for general unhappiness. In this situation, it serves you better to step back for a moment and do a gut check on the person to see if what he or she is saying intuitively "feels" right. You may gain some intuitive insights into the real issue. You might suddenly sense the person's insecurity and realize that you have inadvertently triggered it by something as simple as forgetting to greet him or her in the morning.

Also, watch out for your sensitivity to another's complaining. It may indicate that you yourself are the victim of your own underlying emotional conflict. Do you overreact if someone complains about your company or some other affiliation? The racing thoughts that often accompany a defensive attitude may clutter your mind and prevent you from reading the person and any hidden agenda clearly—perhaps the person is jealous of you. Your defensiveness could be a sign that you identify your own self-worth too closely with the company for which you work. This can lead you to take complaints about your company personally, which, in turn, can put you in a reactive and nonintuitive frame of mind. Realizing this can help you maintain your equilibrium, allowing you to gain insight into, rather than be taken in by, your attacker.

Here's another tip that works well in a situation like this: Analyze whether your feelings change depending on who is complaining. You may be unthreatened by something a friend says, but react poorly to the same words spoken by a stranger at a party. If there is a difference, try to identify why the same complaint makes you feel differently. You may locate an emotional hot button. If, as I have suggested, you root your self-worth too much in your affiliations rather than in who you are, then hearing a stranger complain about your company may tarnish the positive image you are trying to project. You may feel less need to impress a friend, who presumably already knows and values you.

Tolerating Someone Else's Emotional Hang-Ups

Tolerating another's emotional hang-ups, and permitting them to create problems for you, can indicate that you yourself harbor emotional conflicts that need to be quieted.

This became all too clear to a client of mine, Sheila N., in her consulting business. A major client of hers called one afternoon and asked her to review a lengthy proposal that he needed for a 10:00 A.M. meeting the following day. Because of the short notice, Sheila needed assistance. Anthony, one of her associates, was available. Although he was a good technical consultant, Anthony had one drawback: He was not particularly reliable when it came to working in the evening. In the past, his social commitments had frequently taken precedence over his business commitments. Since it was difficult to find experienced people, Sheila overlooked this fact.

As soon as Sheila finished talking to her client, she called Anthony into her office. She explained the situation, and asked him if he had time that evening to devote to this new project. She impressed on him the importance of the client and the urgency of the work. Anthony said that he had a date that evening, but that he would cut it short and work through the night, if necessary, to review the financial aspects of the proposal. Anthony's problem was that he needed to be liked by everyone and had a tendency to tell people what they wanted to hear. Sheila knew this, and asked if he was absolutely sure he could meet the deadline. He assured her that he would get it done. In fact, he said, he would have Marilyn, his secretary, come in at 7:00 A.M. the next morning to start typing any necessary revisions. Although Sheila had a "bad gut" about his assurance, she ignored it and took Anthony at his word.

The next day Sheila was in the office by 7:00 A.M. Anthony was already at his desk, furiously working away on his computer. At first, Sheila was relieved. Then she asked him how it was going, and he told her, somewhat sheepishly, that he had just started on his portion of the proposal and would need at least five more hours to complete his financial review. "You know how the guys are," he said. "They want to party even if you tell them you are under pressure to get some work out for a client!" He said that by the time he got home, he was too tired to concentrate. Even with Sheila's help, the job couldn't be completed by the deadline. The client was very unhappy.

Let's take a look at the situation from an emotional point of view. Sheila's consulting business frequently required late-night efforts. From time to time, Anthony had been asked to work late when this occurred, but no more than once every few months. He had created similar problems before. He could never seem to discipline himself when he had distractions, especially social ones. His lack of discipline always seemed to get in the way of his work effort. Obviously, confronting Anthony and getting an assurance from him that he would do the job was not the answer. He couldn't say no to Sheila or to his pals. Because Anthony had a driving need to be liked, he was always trying to accommodate others. The need to accommodate actually blinded Anthony to the consequences of making too many commitments. This was his pattern. His ingratiating nature was his downfall.

Anthony had an obvious emotional roadblock to his success in business. When it affected Sheila and others who relied on him, the problem became theirs as well. Sheila's problem was continuing to rely on someone who was patently unreliable, even though her gut feelings told her not to.

What would you do in such a situation? Have you ever been involved in a similar situation? If so, what did you do? If your response to this type of business problem was, or would be, to complain continually, month after month, to others about how unreliable Anthony was, you may be dealing with an emotional roadblock of your own. Tolerating a problem like this in someone else is a clue to an underlying emotional issue that blocks your ability to sense what the right course of action should be.

Embarrassment

Experiencing embarrassment or the fear of embarrassment in certain situations can also be a clue to hidden emotional conflict. For example, feeling embarrassed if you have to stand up and speak publicly may signal a deeper conflict that obscures intuition.

—A Test—

Does Embarrassment Unduly Influence You?

Is the prospect of embarrassment an issue you need to be aware of in your business life? Consider this hypothetical business situation.

Suppose you began working for a company one week ago and just completed a lengthy report for your boss. You read and reread the report to make sure it was perfect. You are now sitting in her office while she is going over it. As she is reading, she pauses and asks the meaning of a particular sentence. Reading it, you realize that several words have been dropped in typing, and the mistake has gone unnoticed. You had worked late the previous evening to finalize the report and missed the mistake because you were tired.

Now ask yourself the following questions:

1. Do you think you would be embarrassed?
2. Would you be hard on yourself for making the mistake?
3. Do you think your relationship with your boss would change for the worse now that this mistake has been made?
4. Would you tell your boss how you felt inside?
5. Do you accept that you will make mistakes from time to time?

If your answer to any of questions 1 through 3 is yes, consider the possibility that your fear of embarrassment, or embarrassment itself, may suggest that you have an inner conflict, perhaps a lack of confidence, that may exclude your intuitive insights when you need them. Accepting that we all make mistakes from time to time, even when we're at our best, can help.

If your answer to question 4 is yes, chances are good that you are not letting the conflict that causes your embarrassment overpower you.

If you answer yes to question 5, it's likely that you experience no overwhelming underlying conflict.

Being Critical of Other People

People who constantly criticize others or situations, even silently, are usually also inwardly criticizing themselves. This type of mental rumination, like any other type of self-generated, emotionally based destructive thinking, will close access to your intuition. So, if you find yourself criticizing others, or life in business, this is your clue that you may be unhappy with yourself in some way. If you find yourself caught up in repeated criticism, see if you can identity any pattern. It will help you determine the conflict that creates the need to criticize. For example, criticizing a certain type of person repeatedly may mean that you actually identify with that type.

Some managers are prone to criticize employees. If this describes you, ask yourself why, if their performance is so poor, you don't fire them. Could it be that keeping someone around who is not doing a good job is a way of ensuring that there is always a ready victim to dump on to momentarily make you feel better about yourself? Or to keep you distracted from other feelings, even those coming though your intuition? When you use others as a crutch to boost your self-image or distract yourself, you lose.

Have you ever run across a man who fires one female assistant after another, telling you that he can't find one who knows what she's doing? Then the personnel department sends him a male assistant. You guessed it: For whatever reason, he can't deal with women. An issue he never resolved in his personal life was resolved for him in this particular business situation. By his never-ending, self-generated dissatisfaction with his female assistants' performance, he was able to distract himself from his discomfort in dealing with these assistants because they were female, but at the expense of access to his intuition.

Job Fantasies

Do you frequently fantasize about how much easier, or more enjoyable, your job or business would be if a particular person, or situation, were different? If you have a difficult boss, do you daydream about how nice it would be if he quit? What about thoughts that you would be happier if you had a nicer office, or were working on the executive floor? Take a moment and think about what would make you happier in your job or business. Do you feel you have the power to change these unsatisfactory elements? If you don't, because the problem (say, a difficult boss) is beyond your control, then consider the possibility that you are choosing to remain in a work environment in which you feel helpless. As your feelings of helplessness escalate, so does your preoccupation with your dilemma, and—that's right—you can bet that once again there's an underlying conflict that you are unable to face, and that (you guessed it again) will block your intuition.

Frustration

It's natural to feel an appropriate level of frustration when you can't get what you want. Excessive or chronic frustration, however, is definitely a clue to an intuition-choking issue.

Some seeming go-getters get overly frustrated when they can't achieve their goals quickly enough. This often leads them to abandon partially completed, and often worthwhile, pursuits. Why do people permit themselves to indulge in manufactured frustration like this? Because it can distract them from having to face and work on personal shortcomings or inner conflicts.

A friend of mine was a pro at the frustration game. Almost every time I had dinner with him, he would tell me he was out to make a million dollars. Over the years, he repeatedly searched for the deal that would do the job for him. He would get involved in a project, but immediately become frustrated if he thought the project wouldn't produce a million dollars virtually overnight. He would then abandon the project and begin looking for another million-dollar baby. Each time I saw him, he was either excited over finding a new project, frustrated because the one he had wasn't bearing fruit fast enough, or extremely frustrated because he was in between deals. He spent years looking for the fast hit, instead of sticking with an endeavor that could eventually satisfy his goals. It ultimately became clear to me that his unconscious motivation was really to keep himself distracted.

If any of this hits home for you, take a good look at your business frustrations. Accept the possibility that you're acting in a self-destructive manner, and relax about it. Frustration is a great clue. Use it to your advantage.

Difficulty in Listening

Setting aside everyday concerns and preoccupations, if you find it difficult to pay attention in business conversations, you could be repressing some form of inner anxiety, such as a fear of looking less than brilliant in a business setting.

—A Test—
Do You Have Trouble Listening?

If you find your mind wandering during conversations, use this as a clue that you may be blocking your intuitive messages.

If the answer to any of the following questions is yes, you may be a problem listener:

1. Do you try to control the subject matter in conversations?
2. Do you give the other party little chance to talk?
3. Do you feel upset when others disagree with you?
4. Are you defensive in conversations?
5. During conversations, do you think about what the other person may be thinking about you?
6. When you cannot understand what is being said, do you avoid asking for clarification?
7. Are you preoccupied with how you may appear to someone during conversations?
8. Do you become angry or anxious for no apparent reason during conversations?
9. Do you agree with people even when you don't understand the point of what is said?

Remember, your inability to follow a conversation results from an emotional block, not lack of intelligence.

Avoiding Pressure

There are people who want to avoid pressure at all costs. They strategize endlessly to avoid business pressures that may make them confront disconcerting inner feelings or conflicts that they need to face in order to grow. Buckling down to meet a business deadline, for example, puts you on the line to perform and is an invitation to possible failure, but it is a fact of business life. Trying to avoid situations that engender uncomfortable feelings wastes energy. And, interestingly, the internal strain you create in trying to avoid business situations that may put you under pressure is usually greater than the pressure you are trying to avoid.

Manufacturing Pressure for Yourself

Some people manufacture pressure, and they are as conflicted as those who try habitually to escape it. You can create pressure for yourself in one of two ways. First, you can worry needlessly about something; e.g., even though you are always on time for work, you put yourself under pressure by worrying that you won't be. Second, you can inflict pressure on yourself through self-destructive acts; e.g., you elect to be chronically late for work even though your boss has you under pressure to get your act together and arrive on time. However you create pressure, the effect is the same: It fills your mind with an intense distraction. Feeling pressured? Dig deep and try to unearth what issues you're running from. Here's how.

—A Technique—
Removing Self-Generated Pressure

If during the day you feel under pressure, here's what to do to put it into its proper perspective so that you can work toward eliminating it:

1. Write down on a note pad all the thoughts that pass through your mind and create pressure.
2. Assess whether the pressure is coming from what you think might happen or from something that is actually occurring.
3. If the pressure is coming from what you think might happen, emphatically say the word *cancel* every time the pressure-creating thought surfaces.
4. If the pressure is coming from your actions or the actions of others, use your intuitive guide to find what actions you can take to eliminate it.

Feeling Bored, Tired, or Generally Uncomfortable

Most of us close our minds when we cannot accept what our feelings or intuition might be telling us. Mental shutdown is often accompanied by fatigue, boredom, or physical or emotional discomfort. When this occurs, consider that there may be intuitive information at your conscious threshold that you've caught a glimpse of, but don't want to acknowledge.

Conclusion

Destructive emotions can interfere with access to your intuitive guide. To clear them from your mind, you must develop a new emotional awareness. And that means first acknowledging your emotional nature, and then bringing what you feel fully into your conscious awareness. When this is difficult, because, for example, an issue has been solidly repressed, look for clues. They will help you to unearth any destructive underlying issues that block your progress.

Chapter 7

Step 3:
Identify Life Illusions

"I hate it if someone says something that's not true and other people believe it."

Bill Clinton,
president of the United States
Quoted in the *Detroit Free Press*

What You See Is Often Not What's There

Your conscious mind translates the information you perceive in a way that is acceptable to you. Did you know that what you see with your physical eyes lands on your retina upside down? But your conscious mind perceives it right side up because that is the way you expect it to be. If your conscious mind can do this, imagine what else you might be turning upside down to make it conform to what you expect, or want. Whether you believe it or not, all of us do this with all types of information, all the time—for a variety of reasons. And it blocks our intuitive workings.

To help you release your full intuitive potential, this chapter explores how you create, and may be led astray by, what you falsely expect—your mistaken beliefs. Your illusions.

Illusions and Your Intuition

We all create illusions—beliefs not founded in fact—about ourselves and the world around us. Sometimes we do so to cope with our fears and anxieties, sometimes to cope with difficult realities, and sometimes, as when we adopt popular opinions or trendy beliefs, simply because we've been told, or chosen, to do so to fit in with people, or life.

Illusions lead us astray in business, and in life. They mislead us and block or distort our intuitive perceptions. When you accept without question the limits imposed on you by human-potential experts, you cripple the development of your innate abilities. All too often, believing that you can't do something because you were told it's not possible is the only roadblock to doing it. Illusions about the world of business, or how the people in it operate, are equally as limiting. They cause you to unconsciously edit, or disregard, intuitive messages, often with powerful, but misplaced, logic, at the expense of your business success. If you're lucky enough to see the truth, it can be a shock. Richard K., a corporate executive turned entrepreneur, related his awakening as a young man in business:

> "Suddenly I discovered that the value system that I was brought up to think existed in business, that everyone is reliable and forthright, was not true. This epiphany was horribly disappointing. But when I came to terms with it, I was better able to get my business needs met."

Another common illusion is that working for someone else, as opposed to being self-employed, means income security. People working for corporations often worry only about doing a good job, and not about whether the corporation's business will be there tomorrow. But, if you think about it, it's easy to see, especially in today's work environment, that a corporate employee's income risks are not much different from an entrepreneur's. If the corporation loses business, the employee's job income is at risk.

When you're caught up in a business illusion, you risk not making progress. Assume that you manage the account for a major client. You may believe, therefore, that your job is totally secure. Invariably this is an illusion. Where's the risk? You believe you're indispensable and may ignore an intuitive impression that your boss is not happy with your performance. If you hadn't dismissed the impression, you would have done something to verify it and, if it proved true, to correct the problem before you were fired.

—An Exercise—

Can You Identify One Business Illusion?

Take a few minutes to see if you can identify one business belief you have that can't be factually substantiated. For example, do you . . .

- Assume that managers have their company's interest in mind?
- Believe that chief executives are bottom-line-oriented?
- Believe that getting ahead in business depends more on office politics than on doing a good job?
- Think large companies provide a more secure future?
- Think education is the key to achieving your business goals?
- Generally feel that management rarely lets its personal needs rise above company business objectives?

If you've identified an illusion, is it one that you use as justification for not being where you want to be in business? If so, you're not alone. As you work with your intuition, you'll learn how illusions mislead you and block your intuitive channel. And you'll see that what you think is holding you back is not what's really holding you back. Once you do, you've taken back your option to succeed.

Business Talk—The Major Source
of Distracting Illusions

If anyone were to ask you why people talk to one another in business, it might be all you could do to keep from laughing. "Communication, of course," might be your answer. Or it might be, "Obviously, we must talk to each other to get things done." There is no doubt that the basic premise of talking is to provide a way to understand one another. It allows you to have your needs met, such as getting food when you're hungry or having someone do a job for you. But if you believe that's all there is to talking, you may be the victim of something I'll call business talk—talk that doesn't convey facts, but is designed to create illusions that benefit the speaker's agenda. When someone tells you, for instance, that he or she does all business deals on a handshake, that statement may be nothing more than a marketing ploy to get you to believe that he or she is honorable. When you buy into someone's business talk, you may ignore or discount intuitive messages that are contrary to the illusion that person has created for you. When you're disappointed by someone's failing to live up to what he or she says, you've probably been a victim of business talk.

When people excel at using business talk to paint impressive pictures, they can often easily enroll others to follow their suggestions. This is a technique used by a number of charismatic business leaders. Although a part of us knows that we cannot always rely on what we're told, those who are able to use business talk effectively can often get their listeners to momentarily suspend their good sense and ignore gut feelings. The chairman of the board who paints a compelling picture of a company's future that is based in part on facts and in part on dreams can often raise far more debt and equity money for the company than one who cannot.

However, don't be too quick to point a disapproving finger at people who successfully use business talk for their personal benefit. Most of us have said what we've felt was necessary, regardless of whether it was the truth, to get what we needed, to protect what we have, or to survive. Can you imagine a businessperson bidding on a project and stating that he or she couldn't guarantee that the outcome would be as requested.

That person would have little chance of winning. Yet, many times it's not possible to know how something will turn out. So what does the businessperson say? Obviously, what he or she needs to say to win the bid, and what the listener wants to hear—that the project can be completed as requested.

In an effort to sell their product or idea, professionals often use illusions—business talk—freely exaggerating, or "puffing," the value of products or services, to achieve their objectives, and they do so without giving it a second thought. Members of the business community, meanwhile, typically understand and accept this as part of the marketing process. In fact, puffing is such an acceptable part of the sales process that the laws in the United States permit salespeople to legally get away with it in some measure—putting the onus for separating realistic claims from exaggerated ones on the buyer.

Consider the following two situations. Imagine that you are in the market for a new car, and you just took up two hours of a salesperson's time getting him or her to tell you all about a car that you initially liked. After the test drive, however, you decide it's not for you. Do you say flatly that you don't like the car? Or do you say that you are very interested, but you want to think about it? If you are not direct, you are playing the talk game— the same one others play on you.

Now imagine that you're a rookie lawyer struggling to build your business. A prospective client who needs a business contract drawn up comes in and asks if you are experienced in drafting commercial contracts. You've never written one before, but the prospective client also mentions that he can provide you with at least $50,000 a year in future business. Do you tell him that you have no contract-writing experience, and risk losing his business? Before you answer, you should know that it's not unheard of for lawyers, or other professionals, to tell prospective clients that they have the appropriate experience when they don't, just to win business, to survive and prosper. If you think you would be hired even if you were honest, consider whether or not you would hire a law firm to negotiate a major computer software contract if the senior partner told you that the firm had never handled such a contract negotiation. Most likely you would not.

There are other types of business talk. You may have been promised a promotion or a stock option that never came through. What about encountering a person who says he or she will call so that you can get together to talk business, and never does? How about the one who tells you he or she has great financial contacts, but doesn't produce them when you need help? If you're like most people in these situations, you've probably thought something was wrong with you, or with your project. If so, you were undoubtedly taken in by business talk. You failed to see that the offer was merely self-serving on the part of the speaker and not intended to assist you.

Politicians manufacture illusions all the time. Many promise the voters whatever is necessary to get their votes, not what they think they can deliver. Even if a politician is honest, competition often forces him or her to play the talk game. All politicians learn early on that honesty can lose the election. So, even a forthright politician may choose to skirt issues that he or she cannot address honestly without risking votes. The voting public knows this about politicians. And in spite of that fact, many accept what is offered—the illusions—especially when what they are being told is what they want to hear.

One reason we're susceptible to illusions is that seeing others for who they really are, including their shortcomings, requires us to accept ourselves for who we really are, along with all of our shortcomings. But in order to progress and prosper, we must do that; that is the price for growth in life and in business. So, never forget, in a business conversation you need to look beyond the words. You must learn to trust your gut.

Using the Illusion of Truth

The manipulative person who is able to convince the listener that he or she is telling the truth, even when this is not the case, can often win in business—at least in the short term. And the person who is able to discern what the listener wants to hear, and then tell that person as much, also has a distinct advantage. You don't have to be a manipulator, however, to play the illusion-of-truth game. You may resort to this when you discover that being skilled at what you do is not always enough to keep you afloat or prospering.

Manipulative people use many techniques to project an aura of believability. They establish rapport with the listener by sharing seemingly intimate details about their lives that may not be true and in fact may be just a tactic used for effect. Some take this even further by adopting a damaged or vulnerable persona. Others identify and take full advantage of our personal neediness by offering what we desperately desire. In any case, when you're seduced by their illusions, your perceptive abilities are hampered. In effect, you participate in setting yourself up. Gut feelings that tell you that someone may not be honest are ignored or rationalized.

Programmed Blindness

One of the most difficult types of illusions to handle arises from something I refer to as *programmed blindness*. Programmed blindness is the inability to see reality because you've been taught by your teachers, parents, or mentors to believe illusions that they have either inherited themselves or unconsciously created to keep their unsettling emotions at bay. Unfortunately, they proffer these illusions to you at a time when you are impressionable and have little reason or experience to question them. You rarely suspect that some of the illusions that they hand you represent an idealism on their part and seldom reflect the way life, business, or people really are. For example, children are commonly taught that success in business comes as a result of education and hard work. Since children rarely question what they're told, they internalize this belief and carry it forward into adulthood. Staying focused on educational pursuits and working long, hard hours, they never sit back to assess whether or not there may be an easier way or a shortcut to achieving what they want. If they did, they might consider it worthwhile, for example, to spend ten minutes a day dreaming up or intuiting an innovative idea they could sell to a product manufacturer that would provide them with ongoing royalty income. In defense of those who perpetuate programmed blindness, in virtually every case, their advice is well intended.

These "truths" you're indoctrinated with can become so deeply buried in your unconscious that you accept them unquestioningly, even though they are not based in reality. They can make you ignore or distrust intuitive messages. To remove them, simply question them.

The Hans Christian Andersen story about the emperor's new clothes that most of us heard as children is a valuable, and possibly unconscious, message about the adult world. The emperor was told by two cheats masquerading as weavers that they could make him uncommonly beautiful clothes. However, they said, the clothes would be invisible to anyone who was stupid or unfit for office. The delighted emperor asked that the clothes be made for him immediately. From time to time, the emperor and his advisors went to check on the tailoring progress. The reason that they could not see the clothes, they all felt, was that they were either stupid or not fit for royal office. It did not occur to a single person that the clothes didn't exist. When the invisible clothes were ready, the emperor put them on and celebrated by calling for a parade. Only when a child in the crowd shouted during the royal procession that the emperor was naked did everyone acknowledge what they had been afraid to admit—the truth.

—A Technique—
Identifying Programmed Blindness

Finding areas of programmed blindness takes effort. The discovery process starts with the questioning of every belief you or others have; and it also requires recognizing any personal need to maintain certain beliefs that have no basis in fact. You may believe that people will treat you fairly if you treat them fairly. A belief of this nature, for which you have no statistical proof, can distort your sense that there may be more to a difficult business situation than appears on the surface. Even worse, adopting such a belief puts you at a distinct disadvantage when the person you are dealing with can put this belief in its proper perspective and you cannot.

Here's a technique to help you uncover any programmed blindness:

The next time you make, or hear, a general statement about something or someone in business, see if it is based in fact. If it is not, but rather is based on something you prefer to feel, then possibly you've hit an area of programmed blindness. Here's a common situation. Many people, when you challenge them about a particular position in business, will say in their defense something like, "It's the way everyone in business does things." Buying into a statement like this could indicate that you've hit on an area of your programmed blindness. The fact is that neither you nor anyone else could possibly know what everyone in business does.

Embracing Lies and Other Illusions to Avoid Discomfort

When the truth makes you uncomfortable, you are susceptible to being taken in by the illusions, or even the outright lies, of those trying to manipulate you, or by illusions of your own making. This may happen even when you know in the back of your mind that you are being misled or are actively misleading yourself. And that can cripple your ability to properly assess a situation or person you're dealing with, or your ability to listen to any intuitive warnings.

The stories about widows and widowers being defrauded of their life savings by a smooth-talking con artist are classic. When we hear them we're appalled at how easily the victims were stripped of their money. We say to ourselves, we could have spotted the con a mile away. We forget, however, that when our emotions are involved, we are equally liable to be taken in by illusions created by an unscrupulous person. Lonely men and women are wide open to the illusions offered by a con artist of the opposite sex who is willing to fulfill their need. If they weren't vulnerable, spotting the deceitfulness of a money-hungry con artist would be easier. Invariably, when it's too late and the truth comes to the surface, many admit that they had, and ignored, intuitive thoughts that something was amiss.

Embracing illusions is not unusual when you are upset. Suppose you're working in a job you hate and the only thing on your mind is finding new employment. If interviews are slow in coming, you may panic. Negative thoughts like "Maybe I'm not going to find a decent job" or "Maybe I'll be stuck in my present position for years" may flood your mind. A pressing need to leave, coupled with increasing doubts about finding a new job, can make you susceptible to misreading new situations and welcoming illusions offered in order to entice you to take a new position. Finding a job, any job, may become more important than finding a good work opportunity. People in this spot usually grab the first offer, overlooking any negatives.

At times we feel forced to create our own illusions in business. A good example of how personal illusions can override business sense is the situation surrounding the beginning of *USA Today: The Television Show* a number of years ago. The program had a bumpy start. The show format blitzed information across the TV screen. This super-fast approach often lost the audience. But everyone involved adopted an our-approach-is-okay attitude. They created an illusion that everything was going along fine. A few staff members knew in their gut that something was wrong, but for a variety of reasons ignored these feelings. As a result, changes that should have been made immediately were delayed. Valuable time was wasted. Money was lost. The show failed miserably. In reporting on the show's difficulties, *The New York Times Magazine* quoted one of the staff members as saying, "Some of us saw what was happening, but no one wanted to hear about it." The staffers eventually admitted that they didn't want to face the possibility that their dream jobs wouldn't continue.

How do you avoid falling into a trap of your own making, and keep your intuitive channel open? Learn to be an emotional outsider. To do this, you must be willing to accept the truth about any situation or person you're involved with no matter how uncomfortable it may be. Remember, having your dreams shattered is financially better than having your pocketbook emptied. New dreams are easy to build, a new bank account or business is not.

—A Test—

Do You Ask Others to Create Illusions for You?

Are you inclined toward inadvertently asking other people to create illusions for you? Here's how to check.

The next time you have a concern about a promotion, a business deal, or an upcoming risky situation, have lunch with someone whom you respect, but who couldn't possibly know the outcome. Wait until you are at least halfway through lunch, and ask the person what he or she thinks will happen in your situation. If the person responds optimistically and you feel better, you may gain some insight into how easily you can be swayed by someone who is possibly telling you what you want to hear.

Attitudes About People

If you enter business with conditioned beliefs about people that are false, you may ignore gut feelings suggesting something different. For example, if you've been taught that unethical behavior has no place in business, you may assume that it is not present even though there is ample evidence—media reports of fraud, stock market manipulation, and other white-collar crimes—telling you a different and more accurate story. So, even though gut feelings may suggest that something is amiss in a particular situation, they may go unnoticed until the losses are quite great, because to acknowledge the harsh reality of unethical behavior may conflict with comforting illusions.

At seminars I conduct, I regularly invite attendees to express their general feelings about the honesty of people in business. Invariably they admit to their conviction that businesspeople are basically honest. Their reason? Believing otherwise would make them too uncomfortable. Here's one attendee's philosophy:

> "I trust everyone until they prove to me that I shouldn't. If I didn't, I'd feel as though I always had to be on guard—something that makes me feel very ill at ease."

Isn't it the disconcerting truth that none of us has any way of knowing if the people we meet in business are honest or not? How do you feel? On first meeting someone, do you take it for granted that he or she is honest? If you believed they weren't, how would you relate differently to them? The point is, there are liars, thieves, and cheats all around you, and, yes, you may even come into contact with a fair number in the course of your business life. This is a painful thought, but a true one. I am not inviting you to be cynical or paranoid in your relationships; I'm simply cautioning you to maintain a neutral attitude when you meet people. Before a person's actions have told you what kind of person he or she is, it is an illusion on your part to attribute good or, for that matter, bad qualities to that person, and doing so could say more about you than it does about her or him.

Take the following test and explore whether or not you harbor general beliefs about people that could prove problematic.

—A Quick Test—

What Are Your Illusions about People?

Take a moment and consider the general beliefs you have about people in business. For example, do you generally think that people:

Are basically honest?
Are free of destructive emotional influences?
Are interested in maximizing profits?
Want to succeed?
Always have their company's best interest in mind?
Will act logically?
In management are generally fair?
Don't cheat on their expense accounts?
Want to make as much money as possible?
Are generally lazy?
Work only to survive?
Are loyal?

A yes to any of these could be a clue to an illusion about people. Interestingly, answering no could signal an illusion also. Why? Because both answers—yes and no—indicate that you make widespread generalizations about others when none of us have any way of really knowing.

When you have illusions about people in general, you may hand unscrupulous people the ability to take advantage of you in business, and dismiss others who could be of help. Your best protection is to remain neutral in your beliefs about new people. Here's a technique that you can use to do that.

—An Unblocking Technique—
Reverse Thinking

Reversing your thinking so that you consider a belief that is opposite to the one you usually hold can offer new insights into a situation. It's a clever trick to help pull the covers off your reasons for maintaining illusions.

For example, imagine that you're negotiating a business contract, and suddenly you come to an impasse with your opponent that baffles you. You rack your brains unsuccessfully to uncover the basis for his or her position. Let's assume that you generally believe that no one in business would be foolish enough to act in a self-destructive manner, and completely disregard his or her best business interests.

Now, reverse your thinking on this belief. For example, take the extreme position that people always act emotionally in business and are totally self-destructive. Assume that this is true of your opponent in this negotiation. Mentally step back for a moment and consider how this notion makes you feel. Angry? Helpless? Anything else? Are you getting the point? Could it be that you need to believe that people are a certain way—in this case, constructive—because thinking otherwise may bring upsetting feelings to the surface. For example, if your opponent is self-destructive, then no amount of solid and logical reasoning will sway her or him. That means that you don't have control, which can be unsettling and your reason for creating the illusion that others are sane and open to your responsible business position.

Being accurate in your assumptions is unimportant. What matters is that reversing your position challenges your belief system and the illusions that may lurk there. This exercise lays the necessary groundwork to allow you to glimpse how erroneous beliefs can limit your perceptions.

Beliefs About Yourself

Illusions about others are bad enough, what can be worse are the illusions you entertain about yourself. Positive or negative, they cloud or obstruct your intuition. All of us engage in self-delusion to some extent. However, holding on tight to beliefs about yourself can mislead you.

Uncover any illusions you might have about yourself and put them in the proper perspective using the following test.

—A Quick Test—
What Are Your Illusions About Yourself?

Do you harbor positive or negative beliefs about yourself that you suspect are not founded in fact? To find out, answer the questions below, which incorporate some of the self-deprecating attitudes people have about themselves that we can all fall prey to.

Do you think you are not:

Good enough?
Smart?
Rich enough?
Attractive?
Lucky?
Perceptive?
Able to hold your own in an argument?
Liked by your peers?

Supported enough by your boss?
Likable?
Funny enough?
Interesting?

A yes to any of the above could indicate that you are devaluing yourself unfairly. If so, this illusion can have serious repercussions in your business life. For example, unfounded feelings of unworthiness can hurt you, especially when it comes to asking for a raise. Undervaluing your contribution might lead you to not ask for the raise you truly deserve. On the other hand, incorrectly overstating your worth to your company can get you the old heave-ho and not the fat bonus check you so wholeheartedly think you deserve.

Thoughts About Business

By now, you should be getting the idea that any type of general belief may be an illusion that can interfere with your intuitive process. It's worth exploring one more type of general beliefs: those about business. Do you, for example, believe that:

- If you work hard, you'll succeed?
- Large companies provide better job security?
- Small companies provide less financial opportunity?
- Business plans are the key to success?
- It's who you know, not what you know, that's important?
- Playing office politics is essential to success?
- Emotions don't belong in business?
- Emotions don't control business decisions?
- If the economy does poorly, so will you?

If so, as with any other type of general belief you create or hold on to, the key to eliminating it is to be vigilant about examining why you cling tightly to it. If it's to make yourself feel emotionally comfortable, beware. The point here is not to worry about the validity of any particular belief, but to recognize it and accept that it exists.

Consider this possibility. Have you ever based a business decision on an illusion you've actively created? Most of us inadvertently do this all too frequently, and hurt our progress in business. Let's assume that you work for a company in which you mistakenly think corporate success is more dependent on a willingness and ability to play office politics—saying and doing whatever is necessary to establish solid relationships with the people who can provide opportunities for you—than on doing a great job. If you overemphasize the politics, you may ignore or discount new business ideas, because you think they are of little value when it comes to making progress in your company. Consequently, you may focus less on improving your job performance and more on buttering everyone up.

What about feeling that a particular business course of action would produce a negative result, causing you to decide not to pursue it? Here's a common predicament. When someone believes that he or she won't get a decent raise, what happens? Rather than explore where the belief comes from and how legitimate it is—the person might be performing excellently, but lack confidence and harbor self-doubt—the person may immediately get angry at the boss, or the company, solely on the basis of the imagined outcome. This reaction in itself can actually cause the person's fear to become a reality. By acting out this hostility, the person may sabotage herself or himself, perhaps by being tardy or otherwise performing poorly. The concern about not getting a raise may be unfounded, but the anxiety it creates is real and can in turn engender real problems. Recognize that inner conflicts may be generating your negative reactions and that it's possible that you have created an illusion—and projected a negative outcome—because you were anxious about dealing with the risk of failure.

Business ventures, where there are few guidelines to follow and many uncertainties, are another area where illusions that impede progress surface. Successful entrepreneurs are able to keep these illusions under control, and, as a result, outdistance others. But many people are unable to do so, and so cannot succeed in their own business. They are easily intimidated when confronted with situations in which they can't identify established criteria for determining their chances of success, and consequently they elect not to get involved with new ventures. They don't realize that a lack of established criteria can be an advantage, because, while digging into the past to try and decide whether or not something will work can be valuable, at times preconceived ideas, guidelines, and past experiences can inhibit a creative and valuable flow of intuitive ideas. Without preconceived notions, you're open to seeing opportunities as they develop. Alternatively, if you are someone whose emotional makeup is such that you cannot tolerate risk, you may inadvertently ensure failure by not daring new ventures. Then you have lost. Sticking with the status quo allows little chance of finding opportunities. But starting something, anything, offers great potential for discovering opportunities. The outcomes may not be what you expect, but encountering the unexpected is often how real success begins. So, don't allow your illusions to determine a course of action, think objectively, and separate fact from fiction. Then permit your intuition to suggest a direction for you.

Eliminating the Influence of Illusions

To eliminate or override the influence illusions may exert on you, you must first let go of any guilt connected with creating these illusions. Do this by accepting that illusions were dumped on you when you were unable to recognize what was happening—when you were figuratively asleep. Next, reexamine the primary reason why you hold on to them. Is it that you have not thought to question them, or that to maintain emotional equilibrium, you are required to embrace them. In the former case, merely questioning the illusion is sufficient to loosen its grip. When it's the latter, however, you must do more.

After identifying the role you've allowed your illusions to assume in your life, the next step is to learn techniques to minimize their effect. Since ingrained life and business illusions can be quite different for each of us, it's impossible to try to specifically identify them all and then explain ways to eliminate them. However, the following general technique will enable you to identify and remove the influence of any illusion by showing you how to quickly separate fact from fiction.

A Technique for Separating Fact From Fiction

Use the following technique to methodically separate fact from fiction in a given situation so that you can identify and eliminate any destructive illusions.

—A Technique—

Separating Fact From Fiction

The next time you are struggling over making a business decision or trying to solve a business problem, do the following:

1. Get a piece of blank paper and draw a line down the center, from top to bottom. Then write down on the left side of the paper every thought that goes through your mind. Don't edit out any thoughts. If you find yourself making judgments about yourself, write these thoughts down as well. For example, if as you write, you feel that you should not think or act in a particular way, make a note of it. Don't overlook a single thought, even if you think it's absolutely irrelevant.

    If nothing comes into your mind when you sit down to write, do not push yourself. Take a break and do something that requires little intellectual effort, such as riding a bike or listening to the radio. Any form of physical activity will work. After an hour or so, go back to your writing and try again. If still nothing seems to come, then write anything down, even if it consists of senseless sentences or a string of unrelated words, such as "John, like, pursue, blue, and I am not happy." Do not worry about sentence structure, spelling, or anything else. The point is just to begin writing words on paper. This will get you started.

2. Once you have finished writing down your thoughts, take at least a thirty-minute break before continuing. After the break, review what you've written, and underline in red ink every thought that you think is based upon an emo-

tional reaction rather than on absolute fact. Do not underline thoughts based upon facts. For example, if you made the decision not to pursue something because a prospective partner told you that he or she didn't want to be involved, this is a thought based upon a fact. That you did not choose to attempt to interest another partner may be based upon your emotions. You may find it difficult at first to know when to make the distinction. If you're not sure whether the thought is based upon a fact or not, underline it.

3. Now reduce each of the underlined thoughts to four words or less. Assume, for example, that you wrote, "I'm concerned about pursuing the idea of going into a retail business partnership with John because if the venture failed, my family would have to give up our lovely house." You might restate this as "Loss of house." The restated thought should be written on the right-hand side of the page opposite your underlined thought. The restating is important because it will help you identify underlying emotional issues that you do not readily see. Don't worry about whether you are correctly restating your original thought. This is unimportant. What is important is to begin the process of trying to identify unconscious emotional issues that cause you to adopt illusions, and learning how to separate fact from illusion. Leave space beneath your restated thought. In this space, see if you can extrapolate a related emotional feeling. For example, "Loss of house" may relate to being embarrassed because it would indicate failure to your friends. If so, write, "Embarrassment" in the space. Then indicate whether this aspect of your decision process is based upon fact or illusion.

4. After you identify any unconscious emotional reason or reasons why you decided not, for example, to pursue a particular business course of action, see if you can find a change in circumstances that would make you alter your decision. In doing this, let your thoughts and ideas flow without judgment. Even if a thought or idea seems ridiculous, write it down. In this sample situation, you might put, "Find outside investor."

Your page would look like this:

THOUGHT	THOUGHT SUMMARY
I'm concerned about pursuing	Loss of house
the idea of going into a retail	UNDERLYING ISSUE
business partnership with John	Embarrassment
because if the venture failed, my	FACT OR ILLUSION
famikly would have to give up	Illusion
our lovely home	CHANGE OF
	CIRCUMSTANCE
	Find outside investor

5. When you've finished, put the paper aside until the next day. When your mind is fresh, review what you've written. As you review, see if any change of circumstance that seemed ridiculous at first can actually be made to happen. For example, assume that you said that you would be emotionally comfortable if someone backed you with $1 million, but you felt there was no way to get it. If you feel you cannot raise the money, and have never tried, reconsider why you think you could not find funding. Thousands of businesspeople do just that all the time. Is it because you do not feel that anyone would make that kind of investment in you? If so, instead of making that decision, let an investor tell you. In the process of trying to raise money, you may intuitively discover how to modify your approach to make it attractive to an investor. Or, you may gain other insights. For example, by looking for money, you will gain valuable experience, or you may come up with another business idea that is better suited to the marketplace. Or you may discover how to increase your chances for raising money on your next idea. Just because you're not able to sell your idea doesn't mean you didn't make progress.

Always keep in mind that business success is not based on intellectually figuring out today what will happen tomorrow. It is based on learning to determine when anticipated outcomes of present decisions are based upon illusions arising from emotional conflicts within yourself, and then using your intuition as a guide.

Conclusion

Illusions can block or distort your intuitive messages. Although it can be uncomfortable, at times, to let go of illusions about yourself, other people, or business, particularly when the source of these illusions is your parents, teachers, or mentors, it is absolutely necessary to do so.

The key to preventing illusions from distorting intuitive messages is to acknowledge that your general inclinations may not be based on fact. And that your beliefs, positive or negative, may have been adopted in order to make you feel comfortable. Remember, illusions create predispositions and prejudices, and they block or twist intuitive awareness. Anytime you're confused by a situation or by someone's statements or behavior, this could be a clue that your illusions about this person are clouding your intuitive perceptions. Don't be apprehensive about consciously acknowledging the truth. By doing so, you may be disappointed, but you'll rarely be confused.

As your awareness level increases, you'll easily let go of any illusions that interfere with your intuitive process. Eliminating illusions is merely a matter of changing how you think—and realizing that how you think often has nothing to do with reality.

Chapter 8

Step 4: Put the Past Into Perspective

"Every time I meet someone who reminds me of a person who took advantage of me, I get angry all over again."

—Jack T.,
advertising agency executive

The business world places a premium on the past. Prior market successes, or failures, are often a critical consideration in making business choices. Employers, for example, generally measure someone's worth solely on the basis of his or her work experience. The past has a never-ending hold on our lives and thinking, something you'll begin to understand in this chapter.

Being Overpowered by Your Past

There's no doubt that the past should play a role in your assessments and decisions. It can provide guidance, and comfort, in making reasonable choices in business—and in life. But it can also cast a shadow on your thinking process, distort your perceptions, and cripple your intuitive abilities. When you look at a friend, for example, you typically don't see that person as he or she really is at the moment; rather, how you see your friend is colored by your past experiences together, and with others.

When you attempt to align your past experiences with future goals, you can block or distort your intuitive sense of a present situation. Have you ever assumed that a new manager was going to be difficult, solely because you've had unfortunate experiences with his or her "type" before? If so, when you look at this person, you see her or him in the context of your past experiences, which can hamper your ability to fairly size up the person you're now dealing with and may destroy or interfere with your ability to establish a working rapport with this person—something that will not be in your best business interest.

Experienced personnel people often hire largely, and sometimes solely, on the basis of a job candidate's educational background, work experience, solid references, and favorable interviews. These can all be solid decision guides, but they may cause the hiring decision maker to ignore intuitive feelings; thus, for example, missing the opportunity to bring on board someone with a unique and valuable background.

Roland K., a successful executive search consultant, describes a dilemma he faced that led to an incorrect decision:

"I interviewed a guy for a general management position at a large metal products company about a year ago. He looked great on paper and interviewed exceptionally well. His references checked out. He was the type of candidate that usually works out. Yet, there was something about him that I couldn't put my finger on that made me uneasy. My gut told me that he was devious, but I had nothing to point to as proof. I shared my feelings with my corporate client, but the head of personnel was very pragmatic. He interviewed the candidate, felt that his background was first rate, and offered him the position. Within a few months, he started manipulating reports so that his performance appeared better than it was. When this was discovered, he was let go."

In this case, Roland's gut feeling was right, but since he was unable to justify his position, his client went with the facts—ultimately a mistake.

At all times, then, one of your intuition development goals should be to keep your past in its proper perspective. To help you understand the effect your past has on your sensing abilities, this chapter provides you with the opportunity to explore what may be a major impediment to your thinking, and intuitive, process.

—A Test—

How Dominant Is the Past for You?

The more influential the past is for you in assessing people or current situations, the greater the blocks to accessing your intuitive messages. The answers to the following questions will help you become aware of the past's power over you.

Do you:

1. Become preoccupied with referring to past experiences when evaluating new situations?
2. Immediately compare new people you meet with people you already know or knew?
3. Always bring up the past in arguments?
4. After a car ride, often have little recollection of the scenery along the way?
5. Resist making job changes even when you know you should?
6. Have difficulty understanding what your boss or a client or co-worker asks you to do when it is first stated?

A yes answer to any of these questions may be a clue that you need to acknowledge the extent to which the past clouds your ability to see things as they are and to access your intuition.

It should be obvious that if you've answered yes to any of questions 1 through 3, the past may be very important in your thinking process.

A yes answer to any of questions 4 through 6 can indicate that you are lost in past thoughts, and when this occurs, it is something you need to examine.

If none of these situations apply to you, be alert to similar clues that indicate that the past might be unduly influencing you.

Seeing Only the Past

Accept as a possibility the idea that when you look at someone or something, you see only the past until you can assess for yourself the effect that the past has on your ability to perceive what's in front of you. Recognizing this possibility is a critical step in learning to become immediately attuned to your intuitive impressions and see the true nature of people and situations.

Initially, this concept—seeing only the past when you observe something or someone—may seem unbelievable. For the most part, we go though life never doubting that our impressions of what we're looking at or dealing with are based on the reality of the moment. More than you may realize, however, what you think you see in front of you—people, situations, and objects—is often distorted by information about the past contained in your conscious and unconscious mind.

Still not convinced that you can be unknowingly blinded by your past? Well, with a little guidance, you can verify this astounding possibility for yourself. The following two exercises can help you gain insight into the influence the past has over you, and the extent to which it is actually an out-of-balance preoccupation for you. Do them both at times when you won't be disturbed.

One more point before you start: Don't concern yourself with why you are doing what you are being asked to do. Just do it and see what happens. The more you need to know about why or how the techniques work, the more likely it is that you'll consciously or unconsciously steer the results.

—Exercise 1—

Seeing How the Past Is Present

Set aside five minutes a day for the next five days and do the following exercise.

Sit in a comfortable chair, close your eyes, and allow yourself to fully relax. If necessary, use the technique explained on page 56.

When you feel very relaxed, open your eyes and slowly and randomly look around the room. As your gaze falls on an object (let's assume a table), say to yourself:

"I only see the past in this table."

Take a few moments to see what thoughts pop into your mind. Don't be in a hurry. Be aware of your thoughts. When they stop flowing, randomly let your gaze move to something else. Repeat the statement slowly, referring now to the new object you're looking at. For example,

"I only see the past in this rug."

Now watch the thoughts that come into your mind. Don't be in a hurry. Be aware of your thoughts. When they stop flowing, randomly let your gaze move to something else.

Spend at least five minutes on this experiment, moving from object to object. Try this experiment every day for one week. See what you experience. See if you can recognize the extent to which you see only the past in the things and people you look at.

If you're not accustomed to letting go intellectually, allowing your thoughts to flow randomly and freely, you may initially feel resistance to doing this experiment. The resistance may surface as a feeling of anxiousness, or your mind may become blank. If so, try again in an hour or so, or the next day.

By persisting, you may discover something quite incredible— that, in fact, you identify with the past virtually every time you look at something or someone. For example, if you tried this experiment at home, when you look at a particular chair, you may have thoughts about where it was purchased, or who was with you when you bought it. Or the chair may remind you of something unrelated to its purchase, such as an old movie or your childhood home. The more you work with this idea, the more you'll realize how clouded your present perception is by past influences that you are not aware of, influences that can distort immediate and present intuitive impressions.

Once you make a breakthrough, you'll find it extraordinarily simple to look at a situation, person, or object, quickly clear your mind of the potential blinding nature of your past memories, and access your intuitive thoughts.

After completing Exercise 1, do the following exercise.

—Exercise 2—

How Preoccupied Are You With the Past?

Set aside a total of nine minutes a day for the next five days and do the following exercise.

This exercise should be done from start to finish with your eyes closed to keep you completely focused on your thoughts. Do it three times in one day, for a period of no longer than three minutes each time.

Sit in a comfortable chair, close your eyes, and relax. Use the relaxation exercise on page 56, if you need to.

When you feel totally relaxed, with your eyes closed, begin this exercise by stating,

"I am now thinking about _____."

Let your thoughts flow freely. Identify the first thought that comes into your mind as the subject of your thought and fill in the blank. For example, if you start to think about a friend of yours— let's call him Fred—state your thought in the following way:

"I am now thinking about Fred."

If you can, let your thoughts flow to something else, and do the same. Assume, for example, that you're thinking about an incident that happened at work yesterday. Say the following:

"I am now thinking about an argument I had with Mary."

Allow as many direct thoughts to surface as possible. At the end of three minutes, say to yourself the following statement, without being concerned over its accuracy:

"It's clear that my mind is overrun with past thoughts."

The point of this exercise is to uncover the extent to which you unknowingly see the present in the light of past connections. The more you work with this idea, the more this will become apparent to you. And this awareness will allow you to quickly eliminate any blocks to your intuition.

Conclusion

The more you are unaware of the influence your past experiences have on your assessment of a current situation, the more likely you are to inadvertently block or distort your intuitive perceptions. The past has an influence on all of us. And there is nothing wrong with that. To fully access your intuition, however, you must know the extent to which the past is in play in any given situation in order to keep it in its proper perspective.

Chapter 9

Step 5:
Learn to Be Present

"Without properly applied self-observation a man will
never understand the connection and correlation
between the various functions of his machine."
—G. I. Gurdjieff, philosopher
Quoted in *In Search of the Miraculous*

Chapters 5 through 8 have helped you to work on clearing yourself of mental static, emotional conflicts, illusions, and the influence of your past. These prevent you from experiencing the reality of the present moment. When you are present, your intuitive
channel is open and clear.

A critical step in accessing your intuition is knowing when
your conscious awareness is in the moment; this is sometimes
referred to as *being present*. At this time you can feel assured that
you have successfully cleared all blocks to your intuition. In this
chapter, you have the opportunity to experience, and thereby
learn to recognize, what it feels like to be present.

Being Present

Undoubtedly, there may be times in business when it is easier or
more comfortable to indulge your unproductive emotional
needs, go along with illusions, or be stuck in the past. You might
wonder what your state of mind would be if you succeeded in

banishing this clutter. Obviously, you would be in the present. You would be totally in the moment—able to see clearly what is in front of you, unfettered by thought or emotional static, illusions, and past influences. And, you may not now be surprised to know, this is the time when your intuitive channel is clear.

Most people are not in the present, but do not understand this. An obvious example of when even you yourself might see in hindsight that you were elsewhere is those times when you realize that you have been miles away, daydreaming while in conversation. Lost in your own thoughts, you missed what was being said to you. On the other hand, if you've ever experienced a major business setback or personal trauma, such as being fired or having your business collapse, then you know how it feels to be suddenly plunged into the present. These shocks are often accompanied by an unparalleled sense of clarity. Suddenly, you may see the futility of your worries, or the senselessness of your self-imposed stress. You have a different, often more sobering, perspective on your existence. And a realistic and healthy one. At these moments, your business perceptions are at their intuitive best.

At first blush, achieving being present may seem to be uncontrollable, considering all the distractions that may swirl around you—it is something that, if it occurs, does so by accident and not design. Looking more closely, however, you will see that there have been times when without realizing it you have put yourself in an environment or circumstances where being present was a natural outcome. Reaching back into your life experiences, undoubtedly you will recall moments when, although you may not have realized it, you were present. At these moments, there were no thoughts in your mind that related to anything other than what you were presently experiencing and your immediate reaction to it. For example, can you recall a moment sitting in a park on a clear day when, looking at the sky, you were engulfed by the depth of its color? At that moment, you may have had a wonderful feeling of warmth or comfort. What about sitting in your office and suddenly being very aware of your surroundings—the furniture around you, the pictures on the wall, and the color and texture of your office carpeting? Your reaction may have been nothing more than a fleeting feeling of relaxation, of your mind emptying of all concerns and thoughts of the past and future. You were present.

As you become more aware of these moments, you will realize how easy it can be to focus on the present—and to see how, when you do, you remove the blocks to your intuitive channel. The next time a business idea jumps into your mind, examine what happens to you immediately before it surfaces—your thoughts and physical and emotional feelings. Chances are good that you'll discover that you are momentarily disconnected from any worries or other preoccupations and are in the moment and physically at ease. For example, an idea may surface in your thoughts while you are taking a shower at the exact moment that you become totally engulfed by the experience and thoughts of the warm water cascading over your neck and back; or while looking down from an airplane flying over the Grand Canyon.

The Roadblock to Being Present

Learning to become present in business may initially be uncomfortable. If you force yourself to be present in business, there may be times when you must accept people or situations that are not to your liking. It may even make you confront your worst fears—that too many of the people you must associate with are ruthless. With this new awareness, the world of business may appear to be a dangerous place. Being present may also cause you to question the basis on which you measure your worth as a person—for example, the sought-after promotion that you think will make you feel worthwhile may suddenly appear not to be the complete answer you assumed it would be.

Letting Go of Control Needs

Not a day goes by that I don't run into someone trying to take control of his or her career, business, or life. Being mentally preoccupied with controlling your life and events in business will prevent you from being present. All your thoughts will be directed toward *forcing* things to be the way you want them to be—a future, not a present, focus. Of course you must have a future goal, but once it is established, you must work in the present to achieve it.

The fascination with achieving control is understandable, because it's easy to believe that lack of control is the source of all our business problems. This belief is reinforced by a never-ending series of talk shows, articles, and seminar offerings suggesting that control and success go hand in hand, and promising to easily teach you how to take charge.

Although there is merit in attempting to learn to control our life in business, this can mislead us into spending time and energy focusing on wrong approaches. For example, many techniques for gaining control, such as so-called power dressing, or choosing clothes that influence others, often fall short of making a substantive difference. When you rely exclusively on suggested tricks and tactics, you invariably and unconsciously cannot be in the moment; all your thoughts go toward what you need to do to gain control or make changes. And you detach from your intuitive guide.

Think about the types of seminars that attract people in business. Their brochures, which promise to teach attendees how to control businesspeople and situations, are very enticing, and they produce good money for their promoters. It's not unusual to see offerings that promise to teach people how to:

- Determine their success profile.
- Make themselves look important, when they're not.
- Handle difficult people.
- Identify bargaining strategies that intimidate opponents.

These seminars can be extremely valuable, as long as you realize that you must take what is said and integrate it with your own experiences, knowledge, and intuitive information. They alone cannot lead you to success, but they can help bring you into the present by, for example, removing blocks caused by the fear of working with difficult people. You must understand that the danger with these seminars and with other educational material or forums promising business success through some form of control over others is that they can further distract you or prevent you from using the power of your own insights and intuition to successfully navigate your business course. Your objective should always be to see how you can take advantage of your inner talents and depend on yourself for answers.

One final thought about control needs. Have you ever met rich or fulfilled people who aren't intimidating or powerful manipulators, such as writers, doctors, salespeople, inventors, or shy business owners? Undoubtedly you have, and you've probably wondered how they've done it without access to the clever and aggressive qualities we are so often told are necessary for success. The answer is easy. They've tuned in to how to progress and meet their needs using whatever latent talents and individual strengths they possess.

Reprogramming Yourself Into the Present

It's practically impossible to describe what you will feel like when you are present. Consequently, you may have difficulty recognizing when you have arrived. If you once experience this state yourself firsthand, however, no other explanation will be necessary. One small breakthrough can pave the way to solid progress.

A simple way to bring yourself into the present is to gently force yourself to change a habit. Start slowly. As the saying goes, "Old habits are hard to break." And for good reason. Breaking old habits forces us out of our emotional comfort zone.

Here's a habit-changing technique that will gently bring you into the present.

—A Technique—
Becoming Present

One of the simplest ways to bring yourself into the present moment is to change the way you do something physically. Doing this requires you to actively concentrate on the act of changing, and will force all present-blocking thoughts from your mind.

Do the following exercise every day for five consecutive days—longer if you are unable to make an awareness breakthrough.

Set aside ten minutes every day for an outdoor morning walk. Before you begin your walk, decide on two changes that you will make to your daily walking pattern. For example, change the speed at which you walk and the direction in which you swing your arms. If you typically walk fast, slow yourself down to half your normal pace. If you walk slowly, double your pace. In addition, swing your arms in a direction opposite to that in which you normally swing them. If you swing your right arm forward as you advance your left leg, swing it forward as you advance your right leg. Initially, this may take some effort, but stick it for the entire ten-minute walk.

A word of advice: Don't expect to make a breakthrough in awareness on the first or second day. You may, but if you don't, be patient. Persist. Just relax. Just walk. You'll suddenly know when it happens. When you're in the present, you'll begin to see things differently. The trees around you may look greener. You may begin to notice the faces of people passing you. You may notice other details you've never been aware of before.

You can also bring yourself into the present by changing other habit patterns or physical functions. For example, if you drive to work, make a point of taking a different route for several days, then go back to your old route for a day. Then repeat the cycle again. You might also try, while relaxing in a chair, consciously blinking your eyes at a different speed for two minutes. For example, hold them closed slightly longer than a normal blink. As you make these changes, see what thoughts go through your mind. Again, plan to devote five days in each effort. In each case, watch for changes in your perceptions of the world around you. For example, you may see details in your surroundings that you have either never seen or not noticed for years.

Any conscious changes in habit or physical activity, particularly ones you never think about making, will bring you into the present. Be creative. Let your intuition guide you. Experiment.

Conclusion

By bringing yourself totally into the moment—being present—you clear the channel so that your intuitive messages can break through. A simple technique for doing this is to change an old way of doing things, such as taking a different route to work. Once you know what's it's like to be present, your job of eliminating thoughts and feelings that block your present perceptions and your intuitive channel becomes easier.

Chapter 10

Step 6:
Verify Your Impressions

"When I don't make the effort to verify my first impressions about people, I often have to waste time digging my way out of avoidable problems."
—Charles G.,
attorney

The final step in developing your intuitive skills is the simplest, but the most important. You must verify the accuracy of every message that you believe comes from your intuition. By so doing, you will be able to assess how you are progressing, which, in turn, will give you the necessary frame of reference to hone your emerging skill. In addition, if you verify the accuracy of your intuitive impressions, you are less likely to dismiss each success as a mere coincidence, and this will give you the confidence to make intuitive development breakthroughs.

A Written Record of Your Impressions

When you experience what appear to be intuitive impressions, even if they seem outlandish, write them down in a notebook reserved for this purpose, which I'll call your intuition diary. For example, list the names of people whom, without apparent reason, you start to think about, gut feelings you have during meetings with people, and impressions that surface about someone's hidden business agenda or emotional state. And keep track of the impressions you have about career choices, business decisions, and issues.

Circumstantial and Situation Patterns

The primary reason for using an intuition diary is to help you identify any circumstances or conditions that, in hindsight, result in distorted intuitive messages or messages that originate from nonintuitive sources, such as fears or anxieties. If you are having difficulty reading someone's emotional state, you may find, when you review the circumstances or conditions surrounding such occurrences, that you see a pattern. These patterns can be clues that will help you uncover any mental or emotional static or interference with your intuitive messaging system.

Pay particular attention to keeping track of your emotional and physical state right before and at the time of these impressions. Are you tense, relaxed, or in a hurry? Doing this will help you determine when impressions might come from nonintuitive sources. You may find that as you're trying to sense someone's mood, you become apprehensive about finding that the person is in a bad mood, particularly if you're uncomfortable being around a person in such a mood. The apprehension may create emotional static that distorts your intuitive information. Or your thoughts may really be initiated by your apprehension, not your intuition.

Confirming Your Impressions—Directly or Indirectly

Direct verification is the easiest way to confirm if any of the messages you are receiving actually originated at your intuitive source. For example, if you sense that someone is holding something back from you in a conversation, ask that person if he or she is telling you everything. But, be aware that the person may not be willing or able to tell you the truth. So, if this person says that you are mistaken, don't immediately think that you are misreading him or her and discount the information. Make a written note of it for later consideration.

If you are unable to verify your impressions directly when dealing with people, try to verify them indirectly. For example, if you sense that someone doesn't like you, try talking discreetly to that person's friends and associates, or look for other ways to indirectly verify your impression. You might read books that give you insights into how people operate in life and in business. One such book is *Games People Play, The Basic Handbook of Transactional Analysis,* written by Dr. Eric Berne and published by Ballantine Books. Other books that are among my favorites are those that instruct you in the art of reading body language or handwriting.

Body Language

Reading body language is an excellent way to indirectly verify your impressions about people. Through these nonverbal messages, people often unconsciously signal their inner thoughts and feelings. Assume that you are negotiating with a person who you sense is unfairly holding back concessions. Look for tension in the person's face and stiffness in his or her body. People often become tense when they are being evasive or attempting to outsmart you. Other clues might include a refusal to make eye contact, fidgeting, or arms folded across the chest.

Two excellent books on how people communicate nonverbally are *Body Language,* written by Julis Fast and published by MJF Books, and *How to Read a Person Like a Book,* written by Gerard I. Nierenberg and Henry H. Calero and published by Barnes & Noble Books.

Handwriting Analysis

My favorite way of verifying an intuitive impression is through graphology, the science of reading a person's handwriting. The pen becomes an instrument through which people transmit their inner state. Some pointers: When a person's handwriting slopes down across the page, it can indicate a negative or depressed state. If, when seeking someone's advice, you sense a lack of cooperation, a quick glance at the person's writing can help confirm your impression.

As a veteran negotiator, I frequently use handwriting clues to verify gut impressions about my opponent. A right-handed person whose letters slant sharply backward is often highly self-centered, with every thought and action based upon what's best for him or her. If such a person's claims of fairness leave me with an uncomfortable gut feeling, it's likely that he or she is lying to me.

I encourage you to pick up a book on the art and science of handwriting analysis. Start out with *Handwriting Analysis: Putting It to Work for You*, written by Andrea McNichol and Jeffrey A. Nelson and published by Contemporary Books.

Conclusion

Your intuitive development requires that you make the effort to verify each intuitive message you receive for accuracy and, when a message is wrong, to analyze why. Doing so not only will help you see when you're getting in the way of your intuition, but, when you're right, will provide continuing support for your efforts in pursuing the development of your intuitive skill.

At this point, you have all the foundation tools necessary to put your emerging skill into actual practice. The next two chapters show you how to synthesize and integrate all that you have learned in order to actively engage your intuition in business.

Part Three

Putting Your Skills to Work

Chapter 11

Sensing Hidden Thoughts and Feelings

"If you bring forth what is within you, what you bring forth will save you. If you do not bring forth what is within you, what you do not bring forth will destroy you."

—Jesus Christ

The Possibilities

Accurately sensing another's thoughts or feelings could give you a decisive advantage in business, allowing you to anticipate and avoid problems and misunderstandings. Despite any discomfort you might incur, you would be clear about where you stand with others, and able to prevent them from manipulating you, as well as avoiding going off in wrong or unprofitable directions.

In this chapter you spend time learning how to hone your intuitive ability to sense the thoughts and feelings of other people, a talent you had access to as a very young child. Developing this aspect of your intuition depends totally and exclusively on your willingness to allow latent qualities—your intense curiosity and your active imagination—to playfully reemerge. If you have never explored using your intuition this way, be prepared to have the limits of your beliefs stretched and to be pushed against the edge of your emotional comfort zone. Your initial impression may be that some of what I tell you is doubtful, out-

rageous, or even impossible. Pay careful attention to these negative reactions. They are your clues to how you may intellectually create unfounded limits for yourself. If an idea seems difficult
to accept, remain open to its possibilities rather than dismissing
it. Being receptive to possibilities assures you that you are not fil-
tering out information or awarenesses about people. And always
remember that unless you are willing to stretch the limits of your
beliefs, you cannot make breakthroughs.

Ambivalence About Sensing Another's Thoughts and Feelings

Many people who are initially receptive to the idea of intuitively sensing what someone may be feeling or thinking find, upon
reflection, that the concept is intriguing as long as no one else is
able to sense their thoughts or feelings. The possibility of having
someone, in effect, get inside their head, and the ramifications of
having their hidden thoughts or feelings revealed, often causes
them to unconsciously dismiss the idea. And it's easy to understand why. If you're a businessperson, entertaining the possibility that someone could sense your thoughts or feelings may
make you quite uncomfortable. The ability to bluff successfully
is often a key to making a sale, getting the job you want, or being
hired for a project. If someone could sense your thoughts, bluff-
ing would no longer be possible.

Your Ability to Sense Thoughts and Feelings

You've probably experienced moments when, without being
told, you knew another's thoughts or feelings; when you've
been able to sense what was on or in someone else's mind. Can
you recall those times when you knew what your spouse or significant other was about to say? What about a co-worker, or a
boss? Have you ever, during a conversation at a party or in a
meeting, suddenly, and almost uncontrollably, blurted out something like, "I know what you're thinking" or "I know what
you're going to say"? Have you ever finished a sentence for
someone before he or she has gotten halfway through it? Or been

somewhere with your spouse, or someone you knew intimately, and, the moment you glanced at that person across the room, known exactly what was running though his or her mind? If so, there is a high likelihood that you were actually intuiting that person's thoughts or feelings. And if you're like most people, you may have dismissed this with a laugh, giving it little, if any, further thought. You may suggest, and rightly so, that a long, shared experience with an intimate means that you know his or her position on most subjects and can effectively anticipate his or her reactions. This may be true, but the next time this happens to you, consider as an alternative the possibility that instead you've somehow made a mind connection—that you actually did access the person's inner thoughts or feelings. The more you consider this as a possibility, the faster you'll eliminate the limiting beliefs that block your intuitive channel.

Thoughts and Feelings That Drop In Without Warning

At times, when your intuitive channel is open, the thoughts and feelings of other people simply flow into your awareness. We discussed the example of Sheila, who walked into a room and suddenly, and for no reason, felt anxious. Her anxiety came from unconsciously sensing her colleague's inner turmoil. Has this ever happened to you when you've walked into a room full of people? If so, you may have been picking up another's thoughts or feelings. The next time this happens immediately walk out of the room. Invariably, you'll find that your anxiety lessens, or even dissipates completely. The old saying, "Out of sight, out of mind" is true.

Accepting this idea will help you actively explore your innate ability to sense the thoughts and feelings of other people. When others think about you, for example, they ring your mind's doorbell. Depending on the extent to which you are mentally home—not distracted or blocked by preoccupations, fears, or anxieties—you may experience a momentary awareness of this person. His or her name may come to your mind unexpectedly. If you're feeling somewhat depressed or overwhelmed, your ability to edit out these intruding messages is weakened, and you may be run over for hours by the thoughts of others, especially if they in turn are overly preoccupied with you.

Being overrun by another's thoughts, and unable to understand what is occurring, can block your ability to clear your mind of these thoughts and feelings. The next time you have an argument with someone, for example, that seems to dominate your thoughts for hours after the incident, consider the possibility that you're intuitively picking up that person's lingering anger, particularly if you find yourself repeatedly attempting to justify why the person had no right to be angry. If this happens, don't struggle with why you cannot seem to stop thinking about the person. Simply take a minute and write down on paper every angry or related thought passing through your mind. The act of consciously focusing on these thoughts will send a signal to the person that you've "heard" him or her. And the person may stop banging on your mind's door to get you to listen. The act of focusing also allows the message to flow through you and dissipate.

The Process of Sensing Thoughts and Feelings

To be able to sense someone's inner thoughts or feelings on demand, you must put into practice everything that you've learned so far. And that means that you must:

- Relax.
- Quiet your mind.
- Direct your attention actively and consciously toward that person.
- Playfully engage your imagination.
- Expect the desired results to happen.
- Allow your thoughts to flow freely, without judgment and resistance—no matter what they are, or how absurd they seem.
- Let go of any expectations about how the person's thoughts or feelings will surface into your consciousness.

Above all, don't make a conscious effort to try to figure out what someone is thinking. This will block your intuitive channel. When you try to make things happen, you put yourself under stress. Stress shuts down your intuitive channel.

Connecting in Person

Whenever you talk to or think about someone, your minds link. Your thoughts connect. Rarely, however, are you consciously aware of it. On a subconscious level, that person's thoughts and feelings may be known to you. Sensing these thoughts is nothing more than being able to bring into your conscious awareness what you know on an unconscious level.

—A Technique—

Sensing Thoughts

Here's how to intuitively sense the thoughts of someone with you:

1. Relax.
2. Fully expect that you will accurately sense the person's thoughts.
3. Focus on listening, not talking. Don't worry about answering or asking questions.
4. If the person is talking, suspend all judgment about what he or she is saying.
5. Clear your mind by identifying and letting go of:
   A. All nonproductive thoughts, such as those based on, or originated through, fears, anxieties, or similar negative sources.
   B. All your destructive feelings.
   C. All illusions, preconceived ideas, or notions about the person, such as beliefs that the person is basically honest.
   D. All thoughts about the past—either your past or that of the person.
   E. All thoughts about the future—either your future or that of the person.

      F. Any resistance you feel to using your intuition. For example, are you doubting your ability to sense the person's thoughts? Or are you feeling guilty, angry, or defensive?

6. Pay attention to the underlying content of what the person is saying (read between the lines) and his or her nonverbal messages. Don't let the literal meaning of what he or she is saying lead you astray.

7. Actively engage your imagination. Mentally ask the person questions about what you want to know, such as, "Tom, are you hiding something from me?" And wait for your intuition to respond.

8. Let your thoughts flow freely—don't dismiss any of them.

9. Identify all body sensations you're experiencing, and determine, by asking yourself questions, what meaning they may have for you.

10. Be alert for every immediate thought and impression. Write each one down, if possible.

11. Verify what you can by looking for immediate and later clues from the person, including his or her nonverbal messages.

12. If you actually ask the person about what you're sensing, don't think you're wrong simply because the person says you are. He or she may not be ready to admit that what you sensed is correct.

Don't miss an opportunity to practice this aspect of your emerging skill. If you're like most people, you've spent a lifetime blocking your sensing ability, and to release it, you must make the necessary effort to reprogram your thinking, to remove all mental and emotional roadblocks. And don't be discouraged if your impressions seem wrong initially. Be patient and learn the process.

A Technique for Uncovering Hidden Agendas

You may not realize how often you subtly sense that someone you're talking to has a hidden agenda, or is trying to manipulate you in some way. Start to pay attention to these occurrences. You might find, for example, that a question, just pops into your conscious mind, seemingly out of nowhere. This can be a valuable clue that you're picking up sixth-sense information that you may be repressing. Trust the clue and look deeper.

—A Technique—

Uncovering Hidden Agendas

Here's a technique to uncover possible hidden agendas when dealing with people. Try it the next time you're in a business or social conversation with someone, particularly if you feel that the person is holding something back from you, or if, without knowing why, you find yourself feeling uncomfortable.

During your conversation, ask yourself such questions as the following:

> "What does this person really want from me?"

> "What is this person trying to accomplish?"

> "Is this person really telling me the truth?"

Trust the *immediate* answers that come into your mind. Your intuition always speaks immediately. Don't try to concoct a second answer that seems more logical, or more appropriate. And don't try to figure out what's behind a particular thought.

Pay attention to any physical sensations you're experiencing during the conversation. You will find that you have a distinct physical feeling each time you focus on someone. Don't try to attach a meaning to any physical sensation during the conversation.

After the conversation, go to a quiet place and write down on a note pad the impressions, thoughts, and physical sensations you experienced during the conversation.

Then, sit quietly and think about the person. "Remember" any physical feeling you experienced. You can call forth this feeling by simply focusing gently on the person. Reconnecting with the physical sensation will enable you to explore what you were sensing about the person at a time when you were perhaps too distracted to pay full attention to it. Freely explore various thoughts. There will be a moment when, as you search for specific information about someone, you'll feel that the thought you have matches the physical feeling. When that occurs, you've intuited the correct answer.

Most of us are so detached from our physical signals that this exercise can be difficult. Getting in touch with them should be a near-term goal. It will pay dividends for you. Don't worry if you have difficulty relating to this concept. Let your subconscious work on it. Accept it as a possibility. There will be a point when you will know how this works.

Once you've done this, look for ways to later verify your thoughts and impressions—for example, observing what the person does or says the next time you see him or her.

Connecting at a Distance

As discussed earlier in this chapter, a major roadblock to sensing the thoughts and feelings of other people can be the general belief that it is not possible. It's hard enough to make the necessary leap of faith to trust your intuitive ability when the person is standing in front of you, but making that leap is even harder when the person is not physically present. However, thoughts and feelings have no boundaries—a distance of two miles is no more a barrier than a distance of two feet. They can be accessed by simply calling the person on your intuition telephone.

In spite of our general cultural disbelief in thought sensing, most of us have heard believable stories about the thought communication between mother and child, or between family members who are physically separated. Incidents abound of people who are startled awake at night by the dream of a distant loved one calling out for help, and who learn shortly thereafter that their dream was a reality—the person was in trouble. The key to sensing the thoughts of someone who is not physically present is to remain open to the possibility that you can do it.

To intuit the thoughts of someone who is not in your physical presence, the steps are similar to those in sensing the thoughts of someone in your physical presence, with a few exceptions. Here's the technique.

—A Technique—

Sensing Distant Thoughts

Here are the specific steps you must follow when you wish to sense the thoughts of someone not in your presence.

1. Relax.
2. Visualize the person. Don't concern yourself with whether your image of the person is exactly like the person. (If you have something belonging to the person, use it as an intuition bridge. Place it in front of you or hold it.)
3. Expect that you can access the person's thoughts and feelings.
4. Allow any and all images of the person, such as what he or she is doing, to pass through your mind.
5. Suspend all judgment about the person.
6. Clear your mind, by identifying and letting go of:
   A. All nonproductive thoughts, such as those based on, or originated through, fears, anxieties, or similar negative sources.
   B. All your destructive feelings.
   C. All illusions, preconceived ideas, or notions about the person, such as beliefs that the person is basically honest.
   D. All thoughts about the past—either your past or that of the person.
   E. All thoughts about the future—either your future or that of the person.
   F. Any resistance you feel to using your intuition. For example, are you doubting your ability to sense the person's thoughts? Or are you feeling guilty, angry, or defensive?
7. Engage your imagination. Mentally ask the person questions, and wait for your intuition to respond.

8. Let your thoughts flow—don't dismiss any of them.
9. Identify all body sensations you're experiencing, and determine, by asking yourself questions, what meaning they may have for you.
10. Be alert for every immediate thought and impression. Write each one down, if possible.
11. If you later see or talk to the person:
    A. Verify what you can by looking for clues from the person, including his or her nonverbal messages.
    B. Don't expect the person to confirm what you've intuited. It may be too uncomfortable or unsettling for him or her to admit anything.

Identifying Someone's Emotional State

In the business arena, we seldom get to choose whom we must work with. Intuiting strategies for approaching and relating well to others can therefore be a valuable tool. Assessing the emotional state of other people can provide useful information for determining what approach must be taken when communicating with them. It's a key to achieving the results you want, and to keeping relationships on a solid and positive basis. An awareness of another person's emotional state is also invaluable in indicating when you may be wasting your time with someone. For example, someone under stress may not respond positively to requests because that person cannot give you her or his full attention. Or, someone with a negative attitude is unlikely to agree with much of what you say, or even participate in a constructive conversation.

—A Technique—
Identifying Someone's Emotional State

Knowing a person's emotional state in advance allows you to formulate an approach that is more likely to get the result you need.

And remember, there is nothing mysterious about using this technique, even though the person is not in your presence. It is simply a way to access your intuition, and the person need not be in front of you for you to use it. Here's what to do.

1. The next time you intend to meet with someone, take a few minutes before your meeting, close your eyes, and think about the person you're about to see. Let your thoughts and feelings flow toward the person, as you would toward a loved one or a person you would reminisce about. Sense his or her body mass. Ask yourself about the person's emotional state. If you're a visual person, picture this person in your mind's eye. Above all, let all thoughts, feelings, and images flow freely. Don't edit any of them.

2. If you feel any resistance or if you are uncomfortable, don't force yourself to continue. If you cannot rid yourself of negative thoughts, such as "I can't do this," try again at a later time, and pick someone else as your focus. Forcing yourself blocks your ability to make an intuitive connection. Eventually, you'll make a breakthrough. And remember, there is no right way to connect with your intuition.

3. Once the connection is made, explore any visual images, knowledge, feelings, or thoughts related to the person you have selected. If what you pick up has no obvious meaning for you, explore and guess at its meaning. For example, if you see the person in an unusual situation, allow your thoughts about why the person is there to flow. Or if you see colors around the person, see if you can attach any emotional meaning to them. You may see a gray haze over someone's head, and as you explore the emotional content or meaning, you may feel that the gray color indicates stress. You may have a knowing sense about the person. You may feel that the person is actually talking to you. You may feel a heaviness as you connect, as though you're mentally holding the person up. Or you may simply have a gut sensation. In the latter case, dwell on your gut feeling for a few moments, while searching your mind for its meaning. Ask questions about the meaning, such as whether or not the feeling suggests that the person is happy. When you hit upon the right answer, it will feel right to you. Trust your conclusion. Explore all your thoughts, feelings, and sensations for as long as it feels necessary. When you've finished, proceed to your meeting.

4. At the meeting, attempt to verify your sense impressions about the person's emotional state by steering the conversation away from business and engaging him or her in small talk, particularly about news events or the economy. Very often, once relaxed, the person will say something that will indicate whether your assessment was correct. Also, pay close attention to the person's facial expression, other body language, skin tone, and muscle tightness. These can readily indicate what someone is experiencing emotionally. Use your common sense. For example, people under stress often look slightly pale or clench their jaw muscles.
5. If you can't verify your impressions, do not conclude that you are wrong, or that you are unable to make this type of intuitive connection. You may be experiencing an intuition block.

Conclusion

There are many times when we actually intuit what someone feels or thinks, often without realizing it, but dismiss the incident as a mere coincidence. If instead you start to pay attention to these occurrences, and also actively make an effort to sense another's thoughts or feelings, you can learn to make this ability available on demand.

Chapter 12

Accessing Intuition for New Business Ideas, Creative Solutions, Solid Predictions, and Creating Your Future

"Imagination is more important than knowledge. For knowledge is limited, whereas imagination embraces the entire world, stimulating progress, giving birth to evolution."

—Albert Einstein,
inventor

In this chapter, you take another step in expanding your intuitive skills . This may, as in Chapter 11, stretch the limits of your belief system. Again, you may find yourself resisting certain ideas and suggestions. Suspend your judgment if this happens. Unblocking and using your innate intuitive ability requires you to think in a nonanalytical, imaginative, and playful way—to entertain possibilities, not the restrictions of absolutes. The suggestions in this chapter are guidelines, offered to assist you in finding your own intuitive style, not specific formulas that must be followed. And you will find your own style, if you are open-minded.

Solving Business Problems

Problems. Problems. Problems. Rarely does a day go by when we're not confronted with at least one, in business or in our personal lives. It might be a difficult situation or an impossible person. In business in particular, problems create opportunities for advancement and financial reward for those who know how to handle them effectively. Being able to solve problems brings peace of mind and confidence, and confidence goes a long way toward ensuring success.

Unfortunately, for many businesspeople, problems create more problems. They slow down their progress through life, or even bring it to an absolute halt, until a solution is found. If you don't agree, pay close attention to the immediate and almost uncontrollable way your mind begins scanning for possible solutions the next time you encounter a problem, and how preoccupied you become until a solution is found. If it's a very difficult problem, or one whose solution is important to your job or business, you may even become obsessed with finding answers, making it difficult to think about anything else until it's solved.

To solve problems, most of us rely on our knowledge base: what we learned in school or through our experience. Because of the fast pace and uncertain and ever-changing face of business today, however, our knowledge base is frequently stretched. This, coupled with the fact that we often don't have enough time to gather necessary information, often forces us to make decisions we're not comfortable with. Accessing your intuitive source can make a difference when this happens. It is a valuable resource.

The Solution Process

The moment you're confronted with a problem, your intuition immediately and automatically engages, searching for solutions and channeling them to the threshold of your conscious mind. To consciously connect with this information, all you have to do is get out of your own way. And that means being alert to all inner resistance to consciously accessing these waiting messages that you may have, something I discussed in earlier chapters.

Here's a technique to solve business problems.

— A Guideline Technique —

Solving Business Problems

The next time you're confronted with a business problem, try the following technique to access your intuition:

1. Immediately stop trying to figure out a solution intellectually.
2. If you've been talking to anyone about the problem, stop doing so while engaging your intuitive process.
3. Identify the problem clearly in your mind by writing it down on a piece of paper.
4. Fold up the paper and put it away—in your desk drawer, pocketbook, or wallet.
5. Consciously turn the problem over, unequivocally and totally, to your intuition for a solution—announce to yourself, for example, "I am turning this problem over to my intuition for an answer."
6. Don't spend a moment more thinking about it. If you find yourself beginning to search for a solution, you have not made the necessary commitment to allow your intuition to take over. You must do so. Have faith in the process.
7. Once you have engaged this process, go about your normal activities.
8. Be patient. Wait for a solution to pop into your mind when it has arrived; it will, often at the most unexpected time. It may take minutes for the solution to arrive, or far longer.

Two important reminders: Throughout the process of engaging your intuition:

1. Pay attention to any negative thoughts you have about being unable to intuit a solution, or any doubts that you have about your intuitive ability. If any surface, immediately say the word *cancel* to yourself.
2. Keep in mind that the only obstacles to using your intuition are those created by your own personal fears, limiting life beliefs, and cultural and socialization processes.

Developing Successful Business Ideas

Good business ideas have immeasurable value. They can spawn careers, be the basis of fast-track job promotions, or even make us independently wealthy. The intermittent automobile windshield wiper; the plastic grocery shopping bag container for homes that allows easy storage and dispensing; the shower caddy that holds shampoo containers, razors, and soap; the baby bottle with a collapsible lining that prevents the ingestion of air along with juice; and the collapsible wire stand that holds lawn trash bags upright so that they can easily be filled are examples of simple ideas that have successfully created solid market niches.

If you've ever wondered how people come up with money-making ideas, you might be quite surprised to know that the process can be quite simple. You don't need any special talent. You can do it on demand and with little effort. Idea generation is part common sense and part intuitive. It's something everyone can learn to do. All you need is life experience and the ability to overcome any inner resistance—thoughts of "I can't do this"—to your intuitive ability.

If you follow two basic steps, ideas will flow. The first is to do what I loosely refer to as foundation research, and the second is to engage your intuition.

Here's a technique you can use.

— A Guideline Technique —
Creating New Business Ideas

Using your intuition to develop new business ideas to create opportunity for yourself or enhance your career progress is easy. The key is to create a specific frame of reference for your intuition, and then allow it to go to work.
The steps are as follows:

The Preparation

1. *Pick Your Subject Area.* You must set the stage for your intuition by selecting a general subject area to work with. I suggest that you pick one in which you have a keen interest or one in which your background could be of assistance. For example, if you love to cook, you might decide to focus your energies on cooking-related products or services. If you're a mechanical engineer you might choose engineering-related products or services. If you love cars, you might direct your attention to automobile-related ideas.
2. *Do Some Basic Research.* Do some basic market research in the general area in which you've chosen to work. See what products are already on the market. Explore what other services are being offered. Read trade publications or inventor magazines. Get as much new information as possible about the area you've selected. This will get your intuitive motor running.
3. *Analyze What You've Found.* Analyze the most successful business ideas you come across. See if you can identify what they have in common. You might discover that they invariably address existing and easily identifiable market problems in a simple and unique way. This will give your intuition a framework to follow.

4. *Make a Mental Note to Avoid Complex Products or Services.* Stay away from complex products or services until intuitively originating ideas becomes second nature to you. This will facilitate your success. It's a known marketing fact that the more complex the product or service, the harder it is to gain customer acceptance—to make the customer sale.

5. *Make a Mental Note Not to Get Too Far Ahead of Your Time.* Plan not to stretch for any ideas or services unless your gut feeling tells you that they have solid, immediate marketing potential. Direct your focus toward significant market problems that might be waiting for a good idea and where prospective customers can, with a simple explanation, see the benefit of your idea or service. It's a proven marketing fact that if a prospective customer is not aware of a problem, if he or she cannot be made aware of the problem quickly, or if the problem is relatively unimportant, there will be strong resistance to any offered solution.

6. *Organize Your Immediate Thoughts in Writing.* Get a note pad and pen, list each idea category you've chosen, and then note in each category all related problems or inconveniences that might confront people that come immediately to mind or that you have thought about in the past. For example, as a manager, you might have always been frustrated because there was no ready way to find qualified consultants to whom you could outsource work projects. Or you might have an immediate thought that solving problems would be a lot easier if you had a network of people in your field with whom you could discuss issues. This step is merely to take advantage of any of your past discovery efforts, awareness, or intuitive insights. These will give you something to build on. If nothing comes into your mind, don't worry. Go on to the next step.

7. *Consider Using an Intuition Bridge.* In your early efforts, select an intuition bridge that will help you connect with your area of interest. For example, you might place a management book on a table in front of you if you're trying to develop new management ideas.

The Process

8. *Pick a Quiet Spot in Which to Work.* Select a comfortable physical location—a place that makes you feel good physically and mentally the moment you arrive, and one where you won't be interrupted by people, telephones, or other distractions. It could be a favorite room in your home or a secluded area of a nearby park or beach.
9. *Get Comfortable.* Find a comfortable place to sit.
10. *Clear Any Mental or Emotional Static.* Relax and quiet your mind. You can use the relaxation technique on page 56.
11. *Casually Review What You've Written.* Casually scan through your written notes. Think superficially about the problems or inconveniences you've identified that are awaiting a solution. Don't try to force any solutions. Simply review everything.
12. *Take a Mental Walk Through Your Idea Work Area.* Let your mind wander over the various subject areas in which you've chosen to work. Actively engage your imagination. The objective now is to allow your intuition to expand upon any existing opportunities that you've already identified, and to develop any areas of opportunity you may not yet have discovered. Try to go beyond what you've already come up with. Take your time. Stay relaxed. Don't hold back any thoughts.

    The essence of many good ideas is a solution that removes daily annoyances or expands our work or leisure time. Attempt to find aspects of, or things in, your life that create petty annoyances, anxieties, or inconveniences. You might, for example, mentally walk through a typical day at work and search for areas in which you would like to reduce your time commitments or increase your productivity and earning potential. Or you might mentally walk though a typical day at home, particularly if you've decided to develop a new household product. Involve yourself in the process. Visualize yourself, for example, getting out of bed, dressing, and so on. See if you can identify anything about your day that makes you impatient, or an existing product that's inconvenient or hard to use. You may see yourself struggling to pry open the spout on a wax-coated milk carton, or to place a plastic garbage bag in your kitchen waste can.

13. *Trust What You've Picked.* When you've identified something that's awaiting a new idea, don't try to analyze whether or not it can form the basis of a successful solution, simply make a written note of it and consciously commit to letting your intuition work on it exclusively to come up with an idea for a solid solution.

14. *Trust Your Intuitive Process.* As soon as you've asked your intuition to take over, make no further conscious effort to come up with an idea. Close your eyes, relax, and wait for something to surface. Give yourself at least ten minutes. If nothing surfaces, resume your normal activities. Your intuition will still be at work for you. If you find yourself daydreaming about what you could possibly come up with before an idea has surfaced, say the word *cancel* and do something that will take your mind off trying to force yourself to come up with an idea. Eventually one will pop into your mind. It may happen when you least expect it to, such as while you're driving home listening to the radio. You must absolutely trust your intuition to deliver what you need, or the process won't work.

15. *Avoid All Inner Pressure.* Above all, don't put yourself under pressure to perform. If at any time during this process you begin to feel anxious or negative, stop for a few minutes. Do something physical. Take a walk or a bike ride. Then begin the process over again by relaxing and quieting your mind. If you're patient in exploring this aspect of your intuitive ability, you will eventually make a breakthrough. And business ideas will flow on demand.

Business Visioning—A Concept for the Twenty-first Century

The idea of "business visioning"—creatively envisioning, with the help of intuition, a desired result—is rapidly gaining interest among businesspeople, particularly in strategic management circles. A company that develops a positive vision for its future business can spark the reality. And the same is true for individuals: Visioning success can help you achieve your career objectives.

A true and effective business vision is multifaceted. It is a powerful tool in helping to make success a reality. When you consider the elements of a solid business vision, it's not hard to see why: A true vision:

- Inspires.
- Is unique.
- Makes marketplace sense.
- Encourages long-term thinking.
- Encourages risk taking.
- Facilitates individual creativity.
- Creates a powerful drive to win.
- Has integrity.

When effectively communicated by a visionary, business visions have an explosive and uncannily motivating effect on those involved. They create a feeling of hope and unquestionable possibility. And in the corporate environment, the visioning process can engage the intuitive powers of everyone in a company without them realizing it.

If you've ever worked for a company with a vision, you've undoubtedly experienced the "something powerful in the air" feeling—an intangible and uplifting exhilaration—the moment you arrived for work. Outsiders visiting your offices may sense the winning energy, and mention something about it to you directly or indirectly, such as asking questions about how the company got started and where it's going. They may even be noticeably uplifted while visiting you. You may also have experienced a similar feeling if you've ever met someone who had a strong personal vision. Typically, when you're around this type of person, you immediately sense that he or she is on a winning path.

One of the most fascinating stories of business vision concerns the development of the Boeing Company's first jumbo jet aircraft, the Boeing 747. Boeing was in financial difficulty, and decided to bet its corporate survival on management's vision of the next-generation aircraft, a widebody jumbo jet. Aircraft traditionalists argued that the envisioned aircraft was too big, that it could never fly safely. The Boeing visionaries were undaunted. They pursued their objective with a passion. The vision was communicated to Boeing employees. The air seemed filled with electricity. Employees became consumed with making this revolutionary aircraft concept a reality. Incredibly, not only did Boeing prove the aircraft traditionalists wrong, but when the plane rolled off the production line, it was an instant marketing success. And the aircraft turned out to have one of the best safety records in airline history,

Steering Your Business Course

The process of business visioning is more than simply putting together traditional management objectives, such as increasing revenues by 15 percent a year. It is creating business goals based upon intuitive, or nonreasoned, approaches that will propel a company, or an individual's career, light-years ahead of traditional thinking. A business vision is an intuited image that a business leader or individual has of a desirable and exciting future. It is the place where he or she wants the department, business, company, or career to be.

A Business Visioning Technique

Here's a technique you can use to create a business vision using your intuitive skills and then translate it into reality.

— A Technique —
Intuiting a Business Future - Visioning

The process of business visioning—creating your business future—is simple. The backbone of the process is accessing your intuition and enlisting the intuitive ability of everyone involved with you to make the vision a reality.

Here's a seven-step guide you can use to create your future business reality.

1. *Identify New Business Trends.* Identify one or more market opportunities, or business directions, that you believe have possibilities. Base your choice upon your experience and knowledge, supplemented by up-to-date information on emerging market and economic trends.

   Determining evolving possibilities may require talking to knowledgeable people to get their latest insights, or doing some market research, such as reviewing industry or trade publications, to identify leading-edge trends. This is where traditional businesspeople often start (and unfortunately, end), and it will kick-start your intuitive process. Your research will give you the necessary foundation to reexamine your business environment from a new perspective. It will free you from any traditional thinking blocks, and make you receptive to business alternatives that have previously eluded you. It will allow you to take a fresh or innovative look at what is in front of you every day. You may, for example, suddenly realize that you can use existing computer technology to produce an interactive computer disk (CD) that provides your computer customers with the ability to identify the source of computer software problems. Make a written note of all possibilities.

2. *Use Your Imagination to Come Up With More Future Business Possibilities.* Once you've completed the first step, your job will be to put this information aside momentarily and engage your imagination to come up with more aggressive business development possibilities. This will help you unblock any thinking rut you've been in. By engaging your imagination, you're engaging your intuition.

   Identify every new or expanded possibility, regardless of how ridiculous it seems or whether or not you think it's financially, technically, or otherwise practical. Be completely free with your thoughts. Your goal is to allow your innate creativity to go to work. Don't let your prior experience, knowledge, or view of reality cause you to edit or dismiss any possibility. For example, it may occur to you to expand the use of the computer disk even further so that your customers could go interactively, step by step, through solving their special software problems.

3. *Immediately Write Your Thoughts Down.* Make a written note of every possibility as it occurs, and then put the information aside momentarily.

4. *Envision Your Ideal Career or Business Environment.* Now create a general vision of where you want your business or career to be, without regard to the opportunities you've identified in Steps 1 and 2. For example, if you own a business, fantasize about where you would like it to be in two years if you knew you couldn't fail in your efforts. Or, if you're a manager, envision where you would like your department to be in one year if you knew there would be no restrictions in your path. Or, if you're on a particular career path, fantasize what you would like to be doing in three years if you knew it was guaranteed. Use your imagination. Don't be conservative or hold back. Have fun with your vision. Be more expansive in your thinking than you've ever dared to be.

   Suspend any inclination to restrain your thoughts. Put aside any resistance you may feel to imagining your ideal end result. It may help at this stage if you pose some questions for yourself, such as:

   - What would be an ideal product, service, or marketing approach?
   - What aspect of my management style could be improved so that success would be guaranteed?
   - How could I restructure my business, or career path, to move dramatically ahead of my competition?
   - If I had an opportunity to join with other people, or another company, to increase my success, what would those people, or that company, look like?

   Write all your thoughts down on your note pad.

5. *Review Everything That You've Come Up With and Make an Integrated Choice.* Your job now is to review every possibility that you've come up with in Steps 1 and 2, and summarize it on a note pad, using the column heading format below. Also note your immediate gut impressions of each.

Reasoned Opportunities	Imagined Opportunities	Gut Impressions
1.	1.	1.
2.	2.	2.
3.	3.	3.
And so on.	And so on.	And so on.

Once you've reviewed everything, based upon your immediate gut feeling, make a decision about what business possibility you will pursue.

6. *Create a Vision Action Plan.* Create a vision action plan to follow, but do it in hindsight. Here's how. Place yourself mentally at a point in the future, at a time when you have achieved what you have envisioned in Step 4 using the business opportunity you've decided to work with from Step 5. Now look back to see how you arrived here. Use your imagination, unrestrained by any considerations or concerns, to see the structures and approaches you used to get to where you are. See the resources and people involved. Write this down. This is your action plan.

7. *Share Your Vision With Other People.* The final step is to enlist other people in your vision, people who can help you achieve your goal. You must effectively communicate your vision to them. In so doing, make sure that you have addressed their personal, financial, and emotional needs. Show them how they will benefit, emotionally and in career or business terms. If you communicate your vision effectively, it will be perceived as a shared objective, not a dictated obligation. Shared visions are powerful because they enlist, and encourage, individual creativity, intuition, and entrepreneurial drive.

Predicting Business Outcomes

History is filled with stories about people who were well known for their uncanny prophecies. Nostradamus, Moses, Ezekiel, and Edgar Cayce are a few of the more colorful examples. And in many cases their predictions were recorded in some of our most revered books—for example, The Book of Revelation in the New Testament, and the Holy Koran. For many of us, prophecy has a mystical aura. However, a true prophecy is simply a *statement of potentials*, and how these potentials may appear in our future. We do have free will, and we can choose to accept, deny, or interfere with these potentials.

The need to predict events or circumstances is a part of our human consciousness, and a deep inner drive. We often feel compelled to grasp patterns in life beyond those resulting from habitual behavior or cause and effect. In fact, rarely does a day go by that we don't actively attempt to predict our future, or willingly listen to others who are offering to do this for us. For example, as businesspeople, we often spend endless hours trying to determine outcomes or industry trends. In our personal lives, we welcome predictions about stock market trends, the economy, the weather, political and military outcomes, and so on. And when we momentarily think the future is assured, we feel comfortable.

We all have the ability to sense, or predict, the future. It's an aspect of our intuitive potential, as is visioning. Predicting is sensing what may happen, as opposed to visioning, which is the creation of a future potential. Predicting can be exciting and, because we have no control over what we may see, frightening. Visioning, in contrast, is not frightening because it creates what we choose to have in the future. But both predicting and visioning have clear and obvious benefits. Feeling confident about where you're going can give you a sense of security and the motivation to get there. In addition, predicting can assist you in considering what adjustments may be advisable to avoid continuing on personal or business paths that could ultimately be destructive.

As you explore your future sensing ability, keep in mind that you do not have innate drives that cannot be fulfilled. But you do have innate drives that you can interfere with or block.

The Predicting Process

Making predictions about the future can be fun, if you don't take yourself too seriously. Learning to do it is a trial-and-error process. Have no doubt that you can do it, but not by exclusively using your analytical, left-brain abilities. And, possibly, not on the first try or the second try, or even after many attempts. But eventually, if you persist and trust that it is possible, you will make a breakthrough. You will be able to use your intuition to predict potentials for the future.

The secret to releasing your ability to predict is to exercise this aspect of your intuitive skill at every possible opportunity, and to use your mistakes to calibrate your skill by watching for patterns to emerge surrounding instances when your predictions were wrong. Pay particular attention to any thought, body sensation, or pattern that surfaces when you make a prediction that turns out to be wrong. You may notice, for example, that the wrong predictions involve events in which you had something emotionally at stake—your self-image or your financial security. In these situations, what you think are predictions may really be wishful or negative thinking. These patterns will help you make the necessary adjustments to increase your accuracy.

In the beginning, use very simple situations and keep track of each prediction by writing it down on a note pad, along with the eventual outcome. Do not discuss what you're doing with anyone. Keep your predictions to yourself, as well as the outcomes. Be very specific about what you're predicting. Put down as many details as possible. Use your imagination to fully explore all aspects of upcoming predictions, as well as the outcomes. And then record the thoughts, both negative and positive, and feelings that pass through your mind during the entire process. The more you know about how your mental process works, the faster you'll be able to eliminate any mental static that could distort or block your intuition.

Here's a technique for exploring your future sensing ability.

— A Technique —

Practicing Your Future Sensing Ability

The best way to develop your skill at predicting is to approach it playfully, so that you don't create inner stress that will block or distort results. Use the following approach:

1. Start with simple predictions, and ones that will have no emotional or financial effect on you. Don't pick situations that you may have the power to influence. For example, if you predict that your business will fail, you run the risk of creating a self-fulfilling prophecy. Instead, try predicting whether a pregnant friend will have a boy or a girl, or whether your single boss will meet that special person and get married in the upcoming year.

2. As you get into the swing of prediction for fun, start to make other predictions—say, about political election outcomes or Far East military actions.

3. Next, start making business predictions, such as the outcome of negotiations that you are not directly involved with, or the mood of a customer or of another employee with whom you don't come into daily contact and whom you plan to meet with next week.

4. You might also attempt to predict the success of a competitor in a new marketing endeavor you've just learned about.

5. Be willing to be wrong so that you can learn to calibrate your ability through trial and error. If you put yourself under pressure to perform accurately the first time you try to predict something, your chances of failing are increased. And if you believe that you must always be right in order to verify your ability, you will fail.

6. Make a conscious effort to recognize, and let go of, all fears, anxieties, and self-imposed pressures.

7. For each prediction, write down the *first thought that comes into your mind.* This is the thought that you must trust.

8. Once you've made a prediction, make a written note of:

   - All stream-of-consciousness thoughts, positive and negative, that pass through your mind.
   - Any body sensations you experience at the time of the prediction.

9. When you find you are wrong, review your notes. See if you can find thoughts or feelings that consistently recur when your predictions are wrong. Do the same when your predictions are right to determine recurring thoughts or

feelings that are present. These notes will help you develop a pattern to calibrate your skill.

Putting It All Together

You now have the tools, awareness, and information necessary to connect with your intuitive nature—to allow your intuition to be a constructive and guiding resource for you, in business and in your personal relationships. As you begin to stretch the limits of your inner beliefs and free your intuitive potential, pay particular attention to those aspects of your thinking that have gotten in your way—your self-limiting emotions, your unfounded life beliefs, and your illusions. Watch for the signs of resistance, and for the signs of progress. Each time you have an intuitive experience, don't discount it. Accept it, and continue to build on each experience until you realize that your intuitive nature is part of your human nature, and that accessing it is as natural as breathing and walking.

Share your thoughts and ideas about intuition. E-mail the author at rlegal@ix.netcom.com.

Index